AF413431

ALSO BY FRANZ WRIGHT

Poetry
F *(2013)*
Kindertotenwald *(2011)*
Wheeling Motel *(2009)*
Earlier Poems *(2007)*
God's Silence *(2006)*
Walking to Martha's Vineyard *(2003)*
The Beforelife *(2001)*
Ill Lit: New & Selected Poems *(1998)*
Rorschach Test *(1995)*
The Night World & the Word Night *(1993)*
Entry in an Unknown Hand *(1989)*
The One Whose Eyes Open When You Close Your Eyes *(1982)*
The Earth Without You *(1980)*
Tapping the White Cane of Solitude *(1976)*

Translations
Buson: Haiku *(2013)*
The Unknown Rilke: Expanded Edition *(1991)*
No Siege Is Absolute: Versions of René Char *(1984)*
The Unknown Rilke *(1983)*
The Life of Mary *(poems by Rainer Maria Rilke, 1981)*
Jarmila. Flies: 10 Prose Poems by Erica Pedretti *(1976)*

Recordings
There's a Light That Enters Houses with No Other House in Sight
(with David Sylvian featuring Christian Fennesz, 2014)
The Kilowatt Hour *(with David Sylvian, Christian Fennesz, and Stephan Mathieu, 2013)*
Readings from Wheeling Motel *(with Daniel Ahearn and Michael Rozon, 2010)*
"Encounter 3 AM," Hungry Bird *(with Eef Barzelay, 2009)*
Franz Wright Reads at Harvard University, Woodberry Poetry Room *(2009)*
The Knopf National Poetry Month Collection *(2007)*

Film
Franz Wright—Last Words *(2019)*

Axe in Blossom

Axe in Blossom

Last Poems & Fragments

FRANZ WRIGHT

Alfred A. Knopf

NEW YORK   2026

A BORZOI BOOK
FIRST HARDCOVER EDITION
PUBLISHED BY ALFRED A. KNOPF 2026

Published by Alfred A. Knopf,
a division of Penguin Random House LLC,
1745 Broadway, New York, NY 10019.

Knopf, Borzoi Books, and the colophon are registered
trademarks of Penguin Random House LLC.

Library of Congress Cataloging-in-Publication Data
Names: Wright, Franz, 1953–2015, author
Title: Axe in blossom : last poems & fragments / Franz Wright.
Other titles: Axe in blossom (Compilation)
Description: New York : Alfred A. Knopf, 2026.
Identifiers: LCCN 2025034525 (print) | LCCN 2025034526 (ebook) |
ISBN 9780307962058 (hardcover) | ISBN 9780307962065 (ebook)
Subjects: LCGFT: Poetry
Classification: LCC PS3573.R5327 A96 2026 (print) | LCC PS3573.R5327 (ebook)
LC record available at https://lccn.loc.gov/2025034525
LC ebook record available at https://lccn.loc.gov/2025034526

penguinrandomhouse.com | aaknopf.com

Printed in Canada
10 9 8 7 6 5 4 3 2 1

The authorized representative in the EU for product safety and compliance is
Penguin Random House Ireland, Morrison Chambers,
32 Nassau Street, Dublin D02 YH68, Ireland,
https://eu-contact.penguin.ie.

He did not say you would not be disheartened and desolate.
He said you would not be overcome.

—JULIAN OF NORWICH

Not even death can dismay or amaze me
Fixed in the certainty of love unchanging.

—T. S. ELIOT

Contents

II

The Raising of Lazarus

III

Somehow I Will Still Know You

Axe in Blossom

WAIT

The unanswering
cold,
like a stepfather
to a silent
child.

And the late light, if that
is what passes
for light.

Wait.

The steplight.

The light that's always
leaving—
instantaneous
voyager

as it arrives

I

Finisterre

OMITTED

If I think I have problems,
I look for the mirror. Or
I stand at the window
and ponder the future
reduced to more or less
three lbs
of haunted
meat.
And it's always
like I never said:
if you don't want something,
wish for it.
Lost
in the beautiful world
I can no longer perceive
but only, now
and then,
imagine
or recall . . .
First the long sinister youth
and then the dying man
who talks to old friends
teachers, doctors
but they don't understand
the way we feel.

As if they weren't already
sufficiently deranged (I am
eighteen) inside this
darkly pre-rain rustling
forest rest stop,
leaving
Brussels. Not far,
from what I can figure,
from that spot where Verlaine
had a last word,
with Rimbaud, who blithely
handed over the *Illuminations'*
only manuscript before
he walked away forever;
where I am
commencing to smoke
my first cigarette, thinking
in somewhat garbled English
and drinking in German
of all things.
And seeing things:
right about now
this modest inn appears
to be turning
into a white city
encircled by
forest, assumed to be endless;
woods from which all explorers
return,
when they do

return, younger.
Younger
and very much
smaller individuals
with no recollection
of which way they came,
their various adventures,
or how it happened
that they appeared here
of all places: the very one
from which they long ago set out.
And this is our job, we the ignorant
and untold, the un-tolled-to-be,
the born forgotten—
to raise them, equip them
for one thing
alone: to
leave. To set out again
and miss nothing,
and love no one.

1971

IN LIEU OF RENT

The infinite clothed in the particular.
(Could this be the same blizzard you and I watched fifteen years ago?)
Telepathy flowing between us like water.

All that must remain unsaid to be expressed.

(And some things that ought to be, unsaid:
for example, there is nothing
more anachronistic
than the avant-garde.)

The eternal this very hour, that was its job;

one-room apartments
made ghastly
in three days,
a life
like a favorite pair of shoes
that never fit
that are never going to fit.

To find and live again
his most disastrous day—
his quest, his rest.

To live again, or never to have lived
his *alcoholocaust.*

Magical inscriptions, black lightning in white space.

INVOLUNTARY DETOX: SMOKING PORCH

Time for one more?

What are you waiting for?

Then come in.
The nicatorium's all yours.

Mind if I stare?

And quit fretting:
haven't said a word
all day, and don't
intend to
now.

Consider yourself completely alone.

Green vesperal rain at the screen

JAMAIS VU

Now that I've grown old betrayed my dreams
become a ghost,
I think for a while I'll return
as a guest
to a childhood room,
where the sun is the sun
once again, and the wind
in the trees is the wind
in the trees—
the summer afternoon
the endless summer
afternoon
of books, the only
happiness.
I won't have written this.
I won't have written any of it.
I will have back the rights
of anonymity:
there will be no reason
from the faceless
from their safe
distance
for the things they say no one ever said to me
in the same room.

Sunlight, peach tree, the stars,
and Elizabeth's face
talking to me
with shy sly brilliance . . .
Oh there is nothing left that you can take from me.

ANNUNCIATION

Then let it be done, said
the girl to the blinding
visitor, according to
your word. What else
are you going to say

right hand held out
as if to
ward off a blow.

So
the Word became flesh

for nine human months. Then
with her still childlike
body,

she uttered it.

THE BREAK

Then he stopped
dead on the sidewalk
astounded
to overhear himself
say quite distinctly
I quit,
in his own words—
be glad you weren't there.
Pandemonium
in the cerebral
combs, unprecedented
mass desertions, solar
flare-ups.
It said
itself
actually;
the lips moved
not, no thought was
taken. With massive finality
and apropos of absolutely
nothing it came,
a cruel blessing,
the ultimate low
not of an organ
made of ice, or a passing
night train
of black holes. He
kept lying there—
what else was he
supposed to do? With watch

pressed to one ear, emitting
a molecular hum. (Ever wonder
how they fit a whole
hive inside one
of them?) Minute
hand starting to disappear,
such was its speed
by now; on his face
an expression
of guarded rapture.
No one could do a thing
for him now. They'd stop,
gaze down
in disgust
and concern, a moment before
they hurried on, or
without looking
adroitly moved
around him, the way you would
dog shit. Invariably
in such cases there is a line
that no one crosses.
You know what
I'm getting at. Mainly
everyone just stands around
and waits for the arrival
of the ambulance; the mind simply stops, nothing,
silence. Then
the most silver,
the tiniest
sound
of a fracture
like that of an ice cube
dropped in vodka

can be heard
around the world;
people freeze
at whatever they're doing, and bow
their minds, those persistent
illusions in pain, or shame. But
all is soon forgotten,
the sunlight appears
all at once like
a great shadow
and floats with the gas-like hush
throughout the twelve spokes,
the brilliant yellow darkness
of the twelve candlelit
hallways forever
abandoned, forever
emanating out from
the one central
hexagonal chamber
so much larger than all
the rest, in which
the young queen lies
dreaming, amazed,
eyes open wide
inside
her lead-lined matchbox
rockingbed,
tits up
dead, immovable
sow, maggot
in color.

So, I thought,
as the door was unlocked
and the landlord disappeared (no,
he actually disappeared)
and I got to examine
the room unobserved.
There it stood
in its gray corner—
the narrow bed, the sheets
the color of old aspirin.
Maybe all this had happened
somewhere inside me
already,
or was just about to.
Is there even a difference?
Familiar,
familiar but not
yet remembered . . .
The little narrow bed.
I had often wondered
where I would find it,
it find me, or
what it would look like.
Don't you?
It was so awful
I couldn't speak. Then
maybe you ought to lie down for a minute, I heard myself
thinking. I mean
if you are having that much trouble
functioning. And when

was the last time
with genuine sorrow
and longing to change
you got on your knees?
I could get some work done
here, I shrugged;
I had done it before.
I would work without cease.
Oh, I would stay awake
if only from horror
at the thought of waking
up here. *Ma,*
a voice spoke from the darkness
in the back seat
where a long thin man lay
his arms crossed
on his chest,
while they cruised slowly up and down
straining to make out the numbers
over unlighted doors,
the midnight doctor's;
in his hurt mind
he was already merging
with a black Mississippi
of mercy, the sweat pouring off him
as though he'd been doused
with a bucket of ice water
as he lay sleeping. "I saw the light,"
they kept screaming. "Do
'I Saw the Light'!"
Ma—there ain't no light.
I don't see no light.

TOMORROW

Blood went on flowing
inside my veins
for the time being. Words

continued to provide
a life, meanwhile
ruining mine. On tv

the same giggling
dolled-up soft porn stars relaying
the day's major news:

of inflicting pain nobody tired.

Christ did not return,
not as child
not as fire.

THEOLOGY

There must be someone else
who wakes disturbed, alone;
too bad we can't talk
on our tiny phone.
Someone hidden from the day

like me, preparing to endure
the resurrection of the body, or
a gentler life to come:
oblivion. Who mutters
in sync with me, You

who came in the midst of the world
not to abolish suffering,
clearly, but
to *take part in it.*
What does this mean?

THE SHOWER

Naked
in that garish buried light
of hotel bathrooms
everywhere, I stopped
and for the first time in nearly a year
slowly turned to face a full-length mirror.
After a minute
I buried my face in my hands.
I considered it anyway, overruled finally
by shame. A crimson moon-size sun
without the slightest warmth
and in whose light things cast no shade
was shining. And times being what they were,
two hired men had just gotten finished
taking the corpse of a nameless slave down
from a cross and were carrying it
by heels and flaccid armpits
toward a large hole;
with a curse of exhaustion
they tossed it on top
of a couple hundred others
just like it, their eyes all shut tight
as though humiliated
by their own gruesome obscenity. Then
they thought of going to drink some wine.
The sun was almost down now, and
it was getting windy on the earth . . .

INDEPENDENCE DAY

Masonic sheep
grazing
on hillsides

in Virginia, appearing there
like mystic
popcorn

in the long Jeffersonian
$2 bill-
tinted twilight

of early
July,

yippee-ki-yay.

Sheep
with human
eyes.

FAVOR

My death is in the second drawer.

While you're standing there would you mind getting me one?

And there should be a couple left in the medicine cabinet,
when I
wake up.
If I
wake up.
If I
wake up
tomorrow.
But I am confused, I thought
today was tomorrow.
If I
wake up
in a second,

on the right side of the mirror.

FINISTERRE

1

One day blank signs appear
on the highway
replacing the old ones
put there to mislead you;
the pretense, even,
of guidance
taken away,
as it always is.
Both doors locked;
the windows immovable.
And you
up to your chin
in—what is it, vodka? You know—
the one that nobody can smell!
No. It's a salt-tasting
water. Of ocean?
Of birth? Not so. It is nothing,
the tears you have wept in a lifetime
like anyone else, the waters of grace:
except in your case, in the course
of what has turned into this
utterly unforeseen and comical longevity—
old Uncle Mr. Friend of Death himself!
Steering and brakes gone,
and choosing this fairly unfortunate
instant the accelerator

appears to be stuck
at one hundred miles per hour,
the road dead straight, mysteriously
vacant and straight.
For now.

2

Was I ever a child?
I can't remember a thing!
I swear to God I look back and I can't see
anything
except accidentally cutting my finger
and watching
the impressive gash healing
before my eyes . . .
then nothing. Then, stretching before me—
it looked like forever,
a time of fantastic simplicity,
clarity. There was one commandment: Go.
Go, and take nothing. Do not have fear
about what you will eat. (What a lot of talk
there is about needing to eat!) Or
where you'll stay. You'll stay.
What difference does it make
where.
I wish that I had died when I was young.
I find no peace in anything
but work, now—
can you imagine?
And when it is gone, only

terror remains.
A punishment, perhaps
and I am all for that!
There is no peace but
at the deep center
of the voice and ice, far
from the looks of derision
and blame that wait
behind my eyes. And
unaware of them
I walk unseeing up and down
my room as on a stage,
indifferent to the audience
I sense in front and all around me.
Oceanic darkness of faces I can't see
for the light. And how should I know
who they are? Friends
I can't locate
and friends who can't, sadly, be
with us today;
a small number
of those
not yet born,
the hall largely vacant.

3

Look the cold windy green
wind of her
eyes
I suddenly hear myself
saying
to the cat
(unrecorded, let's hope): for

a moment become
the glad bodiless
sentience, the
I
I once aspired to, one
single roseglowing
cloud
to the north, sailing out;
a still-daytime
three-quarters moon,
the first snowflakes, swirling
like the unseeable
particles
out of which they are made,
but why? Those particles
born with the undisobeyable drive
and energy to change,
soon, into
something very different.
Why words for them given
and they themselves taken away?
Why to me, from so far, did you call—
tap on my window,
my shoulder. You spoke (it
is hardly the term),
and I left
wherever I lived, so to speak
and whoever I
happened to be with, even
my lonely wife. All at once
you got in touch
quite unmistakably,
whatever you are. And as always
I was prepared

to obey, but
why?
Why
was I filled with such love,
when it was the law
that I be alone.

THE RULE

1

Father trellis of my voice (or noose) abruptly vanished—

2

I wear this razory fishhook
of crucifix.
Look.

How it helps me
keep my head
down,

down with shame,
the glory
and shame

see this frail weightless chain:

there is another
like it.
Sometimes
my neck feels
like it's
breaking—

It hangs right here
near the heart's
hidden room

where a table is set for me
not

a dark bar.
No more
that pointless horror.

Weightless frail
chain
massive iron
seaweed and
barnacle-bearded anchor—

You may peek from your door toward dawn
and see me attempting to make it
to the end of the hallway

to the restroom
bent double,
gasping
for air in small sips

but I will be there, table set,
for three,
the unseen
host, then me
there to meet my own

glorified body

who does resemble me
in a vague way,
but is not particularly radiant

or splendid: he is ugly,
as though he had been crying all his life

that can't be my soul
people scream
when they first see it

HEAVEN

I've packed
and have nothing to do
but switch off the lamp
and lie down in the blue darkness
and look at the snow.
There is a heaven.
Death
But getting there.
You can't
just say the word.
A blizzard.
I can't see
a single jogger on the street,
a single light on.
I know they're out there, though.
The fittest
drinking their coffee—
basking
in its arctic blue screen;
winter dawn filling the rooms where they sit
unaghast . . .
There is a heaven.
But getting there. You can't
just say the word.
It's Monday
in the world
and time to go. Me,
I'll go when I am told
I'll go
when they're good and ready.

I'm packed and have nothing to do
but lie down and look at the snow.
Which is something
I am good at,
something I enjoy.
Probably, I'll die like this
a long time ago.

It was finished.
He happened to glance at his watch
like the doctor who pronounces time of death.
Then he got undressed and went to bed.

He could hear the wind blowing outside
and lay perfectly still for a while,
his eyes closed in the darkness,
and thought about what he had written.

He wished he could have been more clear,
it was all so clear to him.
So he was twice alone.
But he was also living twice.

A couple hours passed and he opened his eyes
And on the whole he was glad to be awake again
although he had never been very good at it
and found it so painful and strange.

Mansion of winter, huge, far, far from finished, through which the snow hurries, swirling and swarming, and all the bees who've disappeared from earth so far—if no one else can see it, that is no concern of mine. Unfinishable. This house goes for about a hundred hours per word, if you move now. If you dare to. If you still dare to do things like breathe, move, &c. Because there will be no such words, no such hours, not anymore. All night I pace the floor squandering more of them; pace until the slowly growing horror of the morning light drives me back to the mattress, the gray sheets, the sixteen hours of sleep I now require and all the people I will meet there, company! I pace back and forth down the brief hallway, I descend the three stories of stairway, then climb it, counting up to the comforting number, the same one every time. From one of four small rooms I pace, avoiding the bathroom of course, there will be no more baths, and I deeply regret that, after my little experiment with electricity. I pace them counterclockwise, never varying, never reversing my progress, I don't know why and have never dared to ask (this and other lifelong questions such as, How long does the present last). Not for me to inquire, I just keep walking. It is my job. For which I am not paid a cent, making it, also, my glory. I move faster, sickened by my immodesty as you might rightly deduce, but no. I simply move more rapidly at times, in a frenzy of anxiety and dread, I cannot tell you why; pursuer or pursued, I wouldn't know. Or slowly, as slowly as the shadow that moves around the sundial of certain dear faces, more intensely avoided, to my mind more terrible than the memory of being happy.

Grotesque insect, old namesake and childhood companion, armored black wingless moth that begins pillaging the already somewhat disordered kitchen the instant the light is switched off, vanishing effortlessly as though through a door in the air the instant it is switched on again. Don't think you're going to wear it out like that. As a matter of fact, the purpose and very essence of its being might be said to manifest itself in the increasing ease with which it eludes apprehension, depending upon the intensity with which it is hunted down. And it makes no difference whether its attitude toward sharing the same space with you is playful or hostile, even sadistic—perhaps it is just lonely and bored. But I'll say it again: once it observes you have noticed it or given any indication its presence is a nuisance, you will very soon find yourself the perpetual loser in a chronic contest of wills. It now appears to exist for no other reason than to irritate you, keep you awake at night, and all in a spirit of mirth in response to your rage and frustration. There is after all something comical in the various ways you've devised to empower it and make it a hundred times more interesting to torment you. When all you would have had to do is ignore it. There are many obvious ways of shutting out its minuscule sounds—what good is that gigantic brain of yours anyway if you refuse to make use of it?—noises nearly inaudible to those who lie down in the dark with clear consciences, tiny disruptions most would not even register. You know very well that on rising the next day you will find everything as it was the night before, at least in appearance. You are in trouble now. It has no need for sleep as it has never really been awake; it is able to go for weeks, even months, without food and subsists very nicely on the crumbs you overlook in your increasingly panicked obsession with order, busily indulging the delusion that you are going to make the place immaculately spotless one of these evenings in preparation for the unleashing of lightning search-and-destroy missions. When you might have been doing something important, something real, or at least sleeping, gaining strength for the hellish duties that will be waiting to ensnare you both from within and without the moment you open your eyes again. Yes, it is you who are very soon going to become the defeated contestant, wrung out, indifferent, barely able to drag yourself away, a lunatic alone in the night turning the light on and off, on and off, as if signaling to someone, without knowing who it might be or what message it is you are so desperately trying to convey. Listen: the ogre is singing softly, too softly and poignantly to be ignored. Or is it listening, patiently listening and waiting to find out how long it will be before you start to scream and throw dishes against the walls! Suddenly it is mid-afternoon, in the myopic winter light. Why are you standing in the kitchen; what do you think you're doing? Nobody knows. You cannot remember the month, or the name of the president, or the city you live in. And you are terribly worried, you are so frightened and mad, and you don't know why. You can't remember, or never really knew. Who knows what you might do in such a state? No one knows what you are liable to do, oh none of them know what you are really capable of, desolate and unlit hour, mute and agreed-to descent. Ghosts of the electrocuted huddled behind the toaster, facing the wall.

An unusually active day lay ahead of him. An unusually upsetting one, too, as we shall soon see. Was he imagining it or preceding events by the width of some desolate shiver, was it not getting clearer by the second that more was going to be required than had previously been anticipated. A lot more. Already a cruel and cataclysmic derailment of the mere will to shower and dress had occurred, not to mention his chances of sailing confidently out to meet head-on any challenge to the successful conclusion of his mission which, in and of itself, has no bearing on our parable, so mind your own business. What you may consider laughably simple can easily prove—to one without resources you beings by sheer chance enjoy—his nightmarish undoing. Desperately, he feigned the lighthearted chagrin that might accompany discovering that you'd misplaced a cup of coffee or a favorite pen; he was feigning harder and harder now. And only a moment ago he had actually begun to look forward to this exceptional event, long planned. Three months indoors is much too long a time for anyone to comfortably put up with. And surely there was nothing fanatical about the distance he routinely if not always promptly covered when traveling on foot, staggering as briskly as possible, the distance between his present place of residence and that branch of the United States Post Office located on the aptly named Main Street of the town in which he was presently living or, to be merely truthful, dying, dying. This post office was located no more than six or seven blocks from where his house stood; it had commonly been his experience that it was quite possible for him to make it there and back in under ninety minutes. He was sure he could do with some sun. And he had intensely looked forward to this opportunity to spread a little light of his own, from a too infrequently drawn upon store of friendliness and goodwill toward the world. Under proper circumstances. High as a rat, in other words. (Local colloquialism.) The problem, from which he has been blessed but dangerously distracted for a second by this delightful reverie, as well as his actual situation came rushing back now with a sickening impact. For there was nothing there. There was nothing at all in the place he alone knew, looked in on occasionally, smiled down on with glee or concern, depending upon the waxing or waning in terms of quantity as well as quality, and sparingly dipped into, no more than genuinely necessary, except when in the unfortunate grip of the mood of extreme celebration. It should have been there, some should, some modest remnant even. He'd known that they were going to be essential. Could it be that he had finally crossed the line and his waves of farewell were actually a beckoning, a welcoming of rapid old age, of the horror of solitary old age, the pit, madness, there are so many things that are worse than death, I think he knew deep down he had taken them himself, and unnecessarily. That no one else entered the room and took them from him while he slept. He was always there, and did not sleep. But the time finally comes when even those most adept at avoidance of prolonged and possibly lethal exposure to reality must cope with the nature of material things. It feels like the flesh being torn from your face, at first. And it's not a matter of if but when. The fact stood there before him as a mountain. They would be there, yes they would, had he himself not used them, every last one, inexplicably. He had used them all, therefore there were none left. And since none were there, none whatsoever, none were there.

ORDER

F stares at the pill. F takes the pill.

Look, look: F is in his right mind again. I'm sure we are all very grateful to the medical-pharmaceutical complex, and I'd like you to join me in giving it a big hand.

Wait just a minute you.

That is, please pause for a moment to think about what you are doing; devote a brief period of fair and objective consideration to what you have done. It is still conceivable, is it not, that, for the time being and many hours to come, there will be no turning back from your having unlocked and opened wide a door to your wrong mind. My God, I think you're right! Maybe we should opt for staying right where we are. Next time, I mean. Next time I suggest we put our heads together. Let us stay home, let's stay in tonight, I mean the next time it's night. Or is it morning? There you go. Now you're talking. No need to roam; you can stay put. On a trial basis, of course. We really ought to experiment a bit with leaving things alone, leaving them the way they came. Well, not leaving them, and certainly not alone. But you know what I mean. I really didn't even have to say it, did I. Look at me when I'm talking to you. I meant seeing as we are one and the same. I'm not going to ask you again. And we'll remain here, right where we are, I swear to God. I'm sorry. I'm really terribly sorry. I get so worried about you sometimes. Forgive me for once, will you! We'll relinquish the reins, turn over the wheel, what matter to whom! What matter if the driver be unseen? Have some faith. Sit the fuck down and don't

move, any of you. Heel. We can go somewhere else later, I'll drive
and you can chase the car. What are you running from anyway?
You could read a book, try out those new Tai Chi moves. Why quit
now, after we've come so far? Reality's a beautiful thing. Dark as it
is there. Blind as we are.

I think I may have told you this already, about five or ten minutes ago, in fact, but I've got to tell somebody, don't I? I notice your phone is often busy. That is why I leave such long and, some might say, circumlocutory messages. There are so many things I need to tell you. I hate having to leave ten, twelve consecutive messages—may I suggest you lengthen the amount of time made available for recording? Anyway, this is how the staggering event took place, I will try to be brief. The other day an ethereal stranger, just a perfectly lovely guy—he looked a bit like the young Merwin—walked straight up to me and without even moving his lips (I continue to half entertain the conviction that it was by way of the imploring yet masterful eyes) said in a soulful, soundless voice, *When you die dolphins armed with lightweight compact automatic assault weapons appear on your right and your left, as well as directly behind you, and guide you to Heaven whether you like it or not.* The things that can happen as a result of merely getting out of bed in the morning. And you do have to get out of bed. Try not getting out of bed in the morning for several consecutive days, then for several weeks. If circumstances, outer and inner, are lined up just right you may be amazed to discover how much easier it is to simply remain in bed, day by day, week in and week out; at several months, you are bound to experience appallingly intense moments of nostalgia for the previous you. It is not unlikely that the previous you will now and then make a last effort to . . . though on deeper reflection the whole thing strikes me as nuts. If the person is already dead, for example, those dolphins have no special power over him. Nor, I suspect, do they seek to. My impression is they are magnanimously willing to overlook our pronounced intellectual inferiority and are quite interested in befriending us . . . Is that what I heard them discussing, maybe not—memory's a funny thing. What's important is that total vigilance be maintained, at any cost, and that the state of the Republic remains completely concealed from Walt Whitman. Otherwise, one of these days he is bound to rise pale-visaged with the resurrection of the wheat when nobody's looking, take a stroll around, get himself a copy of the old Brooklyn paper he worked on or some modern-day equivalent, and end up shooting himself in the head. And remember: if you think you feel confused, spare a thought for the sick and weary author. There are so many things, good things, he would like to tell you; he wishes he could take you by the hand and show you some things you might never have imagined. But dreary logic commands he make some effort to appease it, or else he'll just tell you what he knows, from his heart, his heart laid bare, and the vantage point of his unique Sitz-im-Høllen. All he knows is he finds himself drawn more and more to that strange woman referred to as Mom; he feels with increasing irritation and guilt that he must see her, sit down with her and talk things out; and he is willing to do this up to, say, every five years or so, in spite of a degree of enthusiasm that might be a match for a man in his seventies setting out to visit an old high school sweetheart who has been spending the past four or five decades in bed, paralyzed from nose to toe on account of a single extremely short-lived lapse in judgment on the part of a temperament normally characterized by the prim and sedate self-restraint of a future dentist. He had run out of things to say years ago, and was accustomed to smiling and nodding agreeably at appropriate moments like someone going deaf in secret. He had hardly known the woman in the first place! And she'd long ceased even to look like herself. What was he supposed to say? What was he doing there anyway? What the hell did he think he was doing there?

MYTH

Gore-splattered, blindly but surely I retrace my steps guided by the weightless thread I'd let unwind behind me as I first left the world of the light and my descent began, may silver scissors sleep. Frail red thread. Scarlet. There is the stench, the eerie roar, more sadness and terror than I think I can bear, in total blindness how should I know what I'm striking out at, my own gigantic heart or fetus probably, I hate to think, my horrible personality maybe; I don't really care, as long as it stops, as long as I am the last one left standing. It all hangs from a thread, dyed blood-red—blood-dyed thread now, the thing slain, or so I once believed. How many times am I going to have to kill it! I reach the final cunning curves, the dusk brightening, my eyes just beginning to open, all recollection of where I had been and returned from fading, face and body no longer painted blood: the picture breaking up, the healing who cares, gradually finally forgetting coming over me mercifully. Good morning! Of course, I'd be more than happy to let you in on some things that persistently trouble me. First, I know that they can't understand me, they never will. Their salaries depend on not understanding me, so many fears and misgivings never once spoken, with deep roots by now, huddling closer together at night in their pens . . .

DARK MATTER

About your final paper there is no need to worry, let me assure you. Once a solitary sentence exists (it may already be written) everything will be contained inside it. A clear and simple phrase will do, sometimes a single word, one giving off that faint but unmistakable light, if you have the eyes for it. It comes from the mind, I suppose; doesn't everything? No, not everything, Professor Loser, but we can take it up later on, hell, we can talk Heraclitus, Aquinas, Descartes, Kant, and Husserl until you turn blue and die. Forgive me. As I was attempting to say, what was I attempting to say, oh yes, it would seem to originate in the mind, that frail radiance, as were you to get down on hands and knees among the dwindling remnant and watch closely with terror and fascination as the very last seed is laid with trembling hand in its tiny grave. But to reiterate for the benefit of those readers who may have been dozing up there in the most remote tiers, I can't see a thing with this damned sun in my eyes— for all I know every last one of you left long ago. Be that as it may, it emanates, our fragile light, at least in part, from mental processes still far from well understood and *Hey—shouldn't you be off flying around the country being fed by your enemies right now?* Pardon me. Pay no attention to him. At the present time, frankly, the manner in which the mind accomplishes this eerie effect or, for that matter, *why,* is anybody's guess. But one would assume this phenomenon has its genesis, so to speak, in the crown and glory of the Creation, that is, one of the six concentric coils of gray slimy matter surrounding, as does the flesh of certain fruits their pit, the ancient reptile core which to this day continues to nestle there malevolently whispering things like "I'll be the last one left standing, don't worry. I'll be the one who writes history thanks. Isn't it time to eat something? The world is for the strong, not those sensitive smarty-pants, we fixed them, and you are my beloved heirs," and so forth. Do not

be distracted, I strongly admonish you. We are not talking about the
defeated; the broken and starved are not under discussion, sympa-
thize as we may, nude, mass-marched to their gaping grave, no, but
this fair candle flame, this poor endangered source of illumination,
be it ever so primitive—early on in my career I perceived it to be a
shade of green, a near-colorless green, perhaps a yellowish green,
yet verging on white somehow, a pure faceless white like the light I
envision lying just beyond the last reaches of the universe, growing
more intense, brighter and brighter, until it is no longer a matter
of arrival but the blissful certainty that you will never have to go
back—excuse me, I seem to have gotten off, in a manner of speak-
ing, at the wrong station, eyes turned from me in pity and horror,
the bird at dawn silenced, the stars fallen and the daughters of song
all grown dim, silver cord so soon loosed, the limp puppets put back
in their dusty box: behold, between one haircut and the next, I am
become one of those I myself have shoved past a thousand times,
recoiling as from a source of contagion, from whose touch I have
flinched; mine now the eyes I avoided, mine the scalding tears, the
outstretched hand and toothless mouth faintly calling for rescue,
and I was the others, as well, ones much like me, bodies I walked
through as if they weren't there, never stopping to wonder, never
caring what irreversible news they might have just received, what
secret cancer they might be host to; I was one of those who are
already lost, irrevocably elsewhere, inhabitants now of that country
where the language is unceasing remorse, and no one can hear it,
and pity is learned far too late, and the tongue is a stone, and no one
is near, and everything is absolutely still, hypothetically. How would
I know? I despise a whiner, I have got to snap out of this, I mean it,
and right this minute, there. *But pray it doesn't happen in winter!* It
was then a great hand was put forth, the Evil One's or God's I never
knew. It touched my mouth and I spoke words, and they must have
been something, for when I knocked nobody answered, and when
I called no one picked up, may dead flies defile their perfumes; and
like a grape-gatherer's the hand passed across the cities and they

were no more, over my limbs it was passed and immediately I was barren and old. This concludes today's lecture, be sure to purchase a t-shirt on your way out and watch for the live album—but wait a minute, I am not finished with the little light. As I progressed toward a degree of mastery, it changed again, and I should know, teller and listener in one. One who cares. Somebody has to. Why? That I couldn't say. Now it seemed to me the color seen by those who crowd around a cradle, the cradles of the supremely fortunate as well as the most hopelessly destitute, each praying they're the only one who notices, and thinking: it has its mother's eyes. Not that one. The mother who is coming, coming closer and closer with every passing moment, the one I have spent my whole life attempting to travel as far from as possible.

Against our better judgment we are going to be giving you a C–, due to the exceptional and unforeseen circumstance of your having long ago fed what was left of your mind to the imaginary pencil sharpener, sole furnishing of your cell (all the more did you cherish it: this did not go unnoticed) and evidently the primary reason, each time you awakened to find all the doors standing open and everyone gone, for your courageous decision to stay. There is no reason for concern. You are in no danger, your degree has in no way been jeopardized by an admittedly sub-average performance. After all. We are talking about two whole years of your life; we are not about to discount those long hours of dissecting what hasn't yet even been born. Infinitesimal as it may be, you have played your part well, never failing to show up, no furtive attempts to withhold come tuition time your muffled mite. You have faithfully kept your eyes fixed on that far off ensemble of light clothes plus map of the Mediterranean's more temperate regions, and that one-way flight, undeterred by unsubstantiated rumors regarding clandestine changes of course while the drugged graduates are sleeping it off in their seat belts, forced two-in-the-morning deplanings at nameless airstrips in the middle of Antarctica—ridiculous. And while it remains highly doubtful that you are employed as an instructor anytime soon—so few are!—you may forever take pride in your contribution to the decades-long labors of many. While research has yet to establish a precise ratio, again and again empirical evidence suggests that the more consumers are baffled by the product, the more applications to learn to produce it pour in, a phenomenon perhaps related to the widely noted observation that there will soon be many more writers than readers in this country. We take no moral stand here, one way or the other. The probability exists, however, that you who are young may yet live to see the near eradication, in the general public, of all interest in serious writing of any kind.

Classroom of black crayons blindly scribbling nothing, nothing without end, identical name diamond-etched in the blue mirror of oxygen; glass branch conducting the world's unheard requiem. Window window in the wall, what's that crossing the sky without sound? Lone bomber with plenty of fuel but no country to land in. So, a few of the not so meek sheep made it. Well, actually a few guys just like these slobbering fools about to be hanged by their tongues. Now the commander in chief is really scared, head in his hands, in his underground office, which is a replica of his aboveground office, precisely the same in every respect, down to the most minute detail, except for the putrid gray bucket and mop in one corner, the tall filing cabinet abandoned in another. Elbows planted on his knees, as best he can the president sits there gigantically at his little wooden desk, a third grader's in 1961, and stares at his remarkably shiny black shoes, which suddenly give the impression of being four or five times farther away than they ought to be, and again he is afraid, and this time it is much worse. The immense woods surrounding the summer camp have just grown, from one second to the next, impenetrably dark, and the last of the other boys' parents came and left with them hours ago.

THE CHOICE

1

Many men must sacrifice the things they dreamed of doing when young in order to endure the various strains of bringing up a child. A sensitive and happy boy, say; one who knows a godlike figure will be standing beside him when he is taken to school for the first time and encouraged to mingle with the local offspring and so will not acquire the habit of fear. But can anyone really respect a man like that? One look at him and you can tell that no one will ever be interested in writing his biography. No, what we're interested in is a person who has come to a terrible crossroads, one long anticipated, one which commands him to make the wrong decision. And think how tragic it is bound to be for my father on that day when he has to sit his six-year-old son down on the couch beside him, massive suitcase at his feet, and deliver his brief anguished speech, something to the effect of still being friends with the boy's mother, who is as if present in the suddenly sunlit room. Yes, the two are still good friends, they "just don't love each other anymore." You didn't hear a lot of that in 1959. He is going to have to leave home now and depart for his own place, location undivulged. He promises to write. He promises a six-year-old child he will write. He keeps his promise, too, making sure as always to retain a carbon copy of the letter. I'll bet you have read it in a book. Isn't it good? I'll bet you never got a letter like that from your father. Do you know I once actually received an anonymous handwritten note from someone who wanted to know what my problem was, a fair enough query. Things started to go wrong when "Many of us"—I still love the thought of that spooky *us* out there—"Many of us," I was sagely informed, "would give a great deal to have had a dad like yours." Is that right. Well, good luck to you then, and watch what you wish for. He rises now to his feet, towering a mile above me and teetering slightly, blind drunk, he

bends down to shake my hand. Have you shaken hands with a six-
year-old boy lately? In heft it might be compared to a little tobacco
pouch, like we used to see, filled with the hollow bones of a sparrow,
cleaned and polished to a translucence which seems to emit a soft
glow from within. He lifts the suitcase, walks straight to the door,
and vanishes without looking back. Leaving the boy to sit there
staring at his hand, which is still warm. I notice I am staring at it
now. The door very softly and far away clicks shut, time ceases; the
boy supposes he ought to begin crying now. But the thought of the
disturbing and humiliating sound he's bound to fill the house with
puts an end to that. Maybe he, too, will rise to his feet, begin walk-
ing toward the schoolyard where he runs into another boy, smaller
and weaker than he is, walks right up to him, and strikes him in the
face, so that his glasses go flying, and then beats him to the ground,
relentlessly beating his face and head to the fascinated and derisive
laughter of his own tormentors as they stand in a huddle around
him. It is all so vivid, he is breathing hard, as if it had already hap-
pened. A sudden inspiration flows over him, introducing itself, in
its way, as the option to die, feel nothing, remain there on the couch
forever, cause Minneapolis to cease existing, and look into the mote-
filled underground sunlight. And that is pretty much what I do.

2 *Still Life Inside Suitcase*

1 pair of socks (quite clean but don't match)
1 750 ml bottle of Kentucky's Finest Jim Beam bourbon whiskey
    (seal inexplicably intact)
1 boxing manual

DELIVERY

1

Three huge knocks, three massive, preemptive assaults on the front door, not the kind you'd be wise to ignore, knocks that know perfectly well you are home. And I am home all right. On what day was I not, these last two years of night. I am lying in bed unable to move, I am halfway down the stairs, I am fully dressed and standing in the dark inside the door before the third knock sounds. I am doing my trick; I am acting like somebody who is not there. Unable to speak, barely able to breathe, I stand still as stone or tree. I listen left. I listen right. Stone or windless tree. Is anything aware of me? Because truly I have felt so much alone. Is God my loneliness? Or is my life, sentience, the word itself, an accidental scum as I know so many believe. As so many fervently believe, growing on the surface of utter nothing. But I am afraid and cannot join in and share their giddy certitudes. Finally, gradually, I turn the lock, I open wide the door, letting night in like a cat. There is something. I feel it in me so much now. It is affectionate, companionable, and kind, I loved it when I was a lonely child, and now that I am a broken man, I think that I would die without it. But there are so many things worse than death. I brace myself, and taking the two determined, dreadful steps into the night, just as I knew I would, gash my shin against the wooden crate half my height, setting off a thumping sound. It feebly thumps with all its might. I'm sitting in the living room facing the crate. Once you guided me there, you took me there and showed me. I am not so sure I want this dog. From here it smells of mange, cataract, and advanced old age. At no point had I sent for this dog, that is all over with. Calls will be made. You will see. By noon tomorrow or the next day at the very latest, this fellow will be winging his way back whence he came smiling like an idiot, still thumping his tail. He will die, he will be buried in the earth or

incinerated. It will be as though he had never been. I have been the
sole mourner at enough backyard funerals. I feel it is dusk. So it will
soon be night. Or light. I like it here. I'm not going anywhere. Ever.

2

No longer the gentle, intelligent, and mournful being who had so
often guided you between worlds, language appeared to be chang-
ing its mind. Then between one moment and the next, between one
haircut and the next, to lose it altogether, silently baring its teeth
and turning very slowly to stare into your eyes with its unseeing
eyes.

3 *The Letter*

He could probably use a little water, maybe a short walk to the end
of the block. In this city with a light on in the distance here and
there. Capital of a failed language. They'll be sending that other box
soon enough, my death's going to have to come and get me. I'm
not lending a hand . . . The light in this room the one light on the
block . . . Let me ask you something. Did I always have to get down
on my hands and knees to exit and enter the door to this place?
I turn to climb my three flights of stairs, and there it is, framed
thoughtfully at the center of the black rubber welcome mat. What
to do. Is it not true that on May 27, 1989, you abandoned hope
entirely? But there are your civic duties to think of. Never met them,
but there are. Finally I bend down, although I must do so very slowly.
I must try to stand up very carefully as well. It's difficult to explain.
And here it is unmistakably in your hand, in the freezing moon-
light, the quatrain of your name and address that exist in this very
city. Now the envelope may well be empty, it may all be a dream I

am having, that is a theory I'm leaning toward; but no, I am holding
a letter. If the envelope is empty, nevertheless, I am holding solid
evidence that you have sent me your address, and that address is in
this city. At this moment, sleeping, you are in this city. I stand up
very carefully. I slowly get to my feet. And by the time I get there, I
have risen from the dead.

II

The Raising of Lazarus

THE RAISING OF LAZARUS

Evidently, this was needed. Because people need
to be screamed at with proof.
But he knew his friends. Before they were
he knew them. And they knew
that he would never leave them
there, desolate. So he let his exhausted eyes close
at first glimpse of the village fringed with tall fig trees—
immediately he found himself in their midst:
here was Martha, sister of the dead
boy. He knew
she would not stray,
as he knew which ones would;
he knew that he would always find her
at his right hand,
and beside her
her sister Mary, the one
a whole world of whores
still stood in a vast circle pointing at,
all were gathered around him. And once again
he began to explain
to bewildered upturned faces
where it was he had to go, and why.
He called them "my friends." The *Logos,*
the *Let there be light,* said
you are my friends. Yet
when he opened his eyes,
he found himself standing apart.
Even the two
slowly backing away, as though
from concern for their good name.

Then he began to hear voices;
whispering
quite distinctly,
or thinking:
Lord,
if you had been here
our friend might not have died.
Now he slowly reached out
into space, as though to
touch a face, and cried. And softly asked
directions to the grave.
He followed behind them preparing
to do what is not done
to that green silent place
where life and death are one.
By then other Brueghelian grotesques
had gathered, toothlessly sneering
across at each another and stalled
at some porpoise or pig stage
of ontogenetic horrorshow, keeping
their own furtive shadowy distances
following
and struggling to keep up
like packs of limping dogs, until
merely to walk down this road
in broad daylight
had begun to feel illegal,
unreal, rehearsal,
test—but for what!
And the filth of desecration
sifting down over him, as a feverish outrage
rose up, contempt
at the glib ease
with which words like "living"

and "being dead"
rolled off their tongues;
and loathing flooded his body
when he hoarsely cried,
"Move the stone!"
"The boy must stink by now,"
someone helpfully suggested. But it was true
that the body had lain in its grave four days.
He heard the voice as if from far away,
beginning to fill with that gesture
which rose through him: no hand that heavy
had ever reached this height, shining
an instant in air. Then
all at once clenching
and cramped—the fingers
shrunk crookedly
into themselves, and irreparably fixed there
like a hand with scars of ghastly
slashing lacerations
and the usual deep sawing
across the wrist's fret
through all major nerves,
the frail hairlike nerves—
so his hand
at the thought
all the dead might return
from that tomb
where the enormous cocoon
of the corpse was beginning to stir.
Yet nobody stood there—
only the one young man,
pale as though thoroughly bled,
stooping at the entrance
and squinting at the light,

picking at his face, loose
strips of rotting shroud.
All that he could think of
was a dark place to lay down
that wasted body.
And tears rolled up his cheeks
and back into his eyes,
and then the eyes began
rolling back into his head . . .
Peter looked across at Jesus
with an expression that seemed to say
You did it, or *What have you done?*
And everyone saw
how their vague and inaccurate
life made room for his once more.

Ronda, 1913

TRANSLATED FROM THE UNFINISHED POEM

OF RAINER MARIA RILKE, 1977–2014

III

Somehow I Will Still Know You

THE KISS, 1

Massive languor, languor hammered;
sentient languor, languor dissected
Deserted, sidereal
fires reignited;
vacated
cocoon
on the newly green
branch;
abandoned and
holier
languor, arise
from love.
The axe is in blossom.
The wood's owl has come home.

THE LAMP, 2

Dark blue evening
street with here and
there a lighted window

of the at home, or
the possibly not.
Yellow circles expanding

concentrically
into the air
and on into space. Lamp

unknowingly molded
in its maker's
image: shining

mind
in its own
darkness (more

and more made up
of that other
vaster

oncoming Night).
Mind coming only so far
into its own night.

THE WORD HOME

BETH

Drifting
down
our street, the first
of November, the silvery
dusk—
That
and the sudden overshadowing

sense of the mystery in the presence
of the most commonplace
things and events in the world, world and word

one at last. Let
alone, let
alone the lights
of home, my
wanderings done.

THE WORLD

Forget the world and then forget
that word.

From things about to disappear
be one who turned away in time.

The instrument can't hear
the music.

And the music cannot change
a thing.

Change your mind, that is
sufficiently improbable.

Change your heart, and do your little time.

VISITORS

1 *The Window*

Lately
I'm drawn to the window
by the sense of someone staring
into it
in hopes of my appearing there
to help him
with his death. By
the very clear impression
that in this very building
a man whose head weighs
around one hundred pounds
has lifted it at last:
he worked with all his might, and now
he's slowly looking
left and right
and everywhere
for me—
he must speak to me
now, and
he will not give up.

2 *Cricket*

Miniature cricket, I saw you before me, my friend describing you
over the phone, chronicling your brief life and fairly gruesome end,
both of us guiltily chuckling. I saw you, saurian creature crouched
there with infinite patience and without the room to turn around
in, without the room to move, inside something resembling an

over-size die of woven bamboo, eye shining, making no sound.
You chirped not. But I am saving my pity for myself, small cricket.
Maybe not tomorrow night, and maybe not three weeks from the
day before yesterday—what difference does it make. Same as you,
and it won't be long, the doomed day will fall, the night dawn

when I will be walking along thinking of something entirely

ELIZABETH'S EYES

Five feet from the ground the sky begins, that plane
of two joined points of darkness surrounded
by the color of the ocean dawn, bright
space of a second infinity
where I want to live forever

T.S.E.

The golden vision reappears

Summer lightning, soundless:
darkness you could read
by, darkness
bright
and brightness dark
above a warred-on city,
at this very instant
in the past, just beyond
the horizon. In Maine
at dawn the little girl
of an ancient love wakes me laughing
and takes me out hunting
wild strawberries under August
lightning; and after many years
some words of yours come back,
a forgotten happiness
turning to a shining
terror encircling me everywhere: right to time's edge,
its ultimate ring
a white blindness, there
at its center the candle
of darkness you work by.
And how strange it is picturing you
setting those words down
when you have never read them
and never will. Lone sail
off Cape Ann, barely visible, lost, glimpsed
and lost in the wind-torn, lit-inwardly
black

sapphire and overcast waves. It is you
as a boy, I think, one hundred years ago.
If I like to think so, why not?
You can't hear me.
I can barely hear
my own mind in this wind, where
the girl's voice is calling from far off, repeating
a name I can't make out,
can't be sure I am hearing at all.

THREE HOMAGES

A Language Regained: In Homage

1 *It's Raining in a Dead Language: To Karl Krolow*

It's raining
again
in a dead language, he writes
at his desk
in the past.
The bindings bound
in gold and brown
darkening,
receding
in their shelves;

buzzing &c.

2 *Axe in Blossom: To Paul Celan*

I hear that the axe is in blossom
and that
we keep waiting
but the one
who can dislodge it never comes—
the poor running in circles
their ribs sticking out,
blood spurting from between their shoulders
I hear about hanged men
brought back to life

by the mere scent of their wives baking bread.
I hear they call life

our only resort.

3 *Let Me Have What the Tree Has (Heaven): To Natan Zach*

Lord let me have what the tree has
what it can never shed,
have it and lose it
again, the blurred lines
preferred by the wind
with the void it stores
from the shapeless
summer nights'
indescribable
darkness. Either
give me back my gladness,
or the courage to think
about how it was lost
Give back my vision,
not what I can see;
let me meet her again,
this time owning nothing
except a few things in the past.
Lord, let me inherit
precisely what I am forbidden.
And let me continue to seek,
although I know it is futile,
the only heaven I could bear: this world,
the one in which she lived her shining life
and in which I'd lost the love of heaven above.

AKECHI'S WIFE

On one occasion Yūgen of Ise Province was offering to share, for
a night or two, the comforts of his home with me when a distant,
bemused look came over his face—I am certain he was completely
unaware of this—as though at the recollection of a joke told him
earlier that day; then, to a degree I would not have thought possible
in one whose normal manner was so formal, that studiedly dour
professorial expression gave way for an instant to one that positively
beamed, illuminated from within by the sound of a beloved voice.
So worn out, not even sure I was on the right road, I forgot myself
awhile watching in weary amazement as his wife came and went,
the two of them giving the impression of having long perfected
some grave and complex dance known only to them, one of accord
and the affection of two people moving hand in hand in the same
direction, both possessed by desire while knowing themselves
to be the source of that desire. But I am so tired, I heard my own
voice say, one of them, that startlingly cruel, intrusive voice I hate,
darkening everything, how sick I am of listening to it, and of having
to go on. But after some time had passed once again I forgot all
about it as I sat there, the witness of this marvel that brought peace
to my heart or, perhaps, a hidden joy of my own, one I had so long
considered extinct. When Yūgen fell on hard times and was dragged
down into the most humiliating poverty, his wife made up her mind
one day to have her long beautiful hair cut short so that she could
sell it and he could afford to invite all their friends to an evening of
laughter and drinking, renga competitions, and the conversation of
those who have known one another for a long time, the kind look
and humorous word that make it seem possible to live again. I think
of her sometimes.

Moon, come down and
come alone. I have to tell you all
about Akechi's wife.

AFTER BASHŌ, 1689

As they carry me out on a stretcher two young men, believing I was born this way, born as a frail elderly man about to die anyway, think nothing of setting me down in the snow so they can stop and watch with interest the ravenous persimmon-colored flames which only minutes ago were my little house, perhaps the last picture I will ever have the heart to do, and a sheaf of pretty good poems, I'm too old to remember them—if I write a poem in the morning, three spontaneous lines it took me most of the night to produce, I may come upon it later that afternoon, mutter under my breath, *Who wrote this? Pretty damned good,* I will say, a little troubled, but at the same time secretly pleased to take note of its glaring immaturities. I stare into the flames. Does this mean all things are removed by only one or two small steps from ash? And was it necessary to take away from some half-mad old poet his small shack, his paints and brushes, the only things that gave him any peace or comfort in this world, when a metaphor to warn against the futility of attachment and the fragility of temporal things was all that was required, when the splendid palace of the Prince still stands in its pearl-like beauty just a short ways down the road? Stunned with anguish I attempt to recite with the Blessed One, *All is on fire, all is burning.* It's not working, and now the extremely realistic illusion of tears rolls down my cheeks silently. Death will find me just as unprepared as when I started out shedding my fear of it as something no more real than shadows in a dream, and evidently there has been no point in all the sufferings and trials of living this long life. Lonely, growing old—the neighbors stare and quickly turn their eyes away when I attempt to greet them in this odd-sounding croak that was once a good voice. No time. No more time to become wise, achieve salvation, or become simple and literal-minded as a child. Words, more words, what horseshit. Shivering with fever, meanwhile, the body is

busy observing, from a much greater distance than usual, big snow-
flakes as they light on my blanket like ash, like white November
moths, and disappear. Where? Won't the mind ever be still, does it
really have to die just to find stillness? I am afraid more often now.
More than ever I am haunted by the lives of the small, brief, power-
less, filthy, and poor. Take the flies. Once I overheard some men
speaking of them as an irritation in the heat, and one of them said
he would gladly hunt down each and every one, until we were no
longer forced to live in the same world. I am always afraid of what
men will do. I am no admirer of flies, but they too love their lives,
the sunlight. People can also be made to disappear; and there are
people who would like nothing better than to see us vanish in large
numbers. And I remembered, so perfect—

> Oh why would you swat them, the poor
> things, forever
> wringing their skinny hands

I have loved words themselves far too much. Sometimes more than
the imperfect and unwieldy things and ideas they represented.
After weeks and months of failure, all at once there the characters
stood—an unheard-of constellation faintly glowing back at me
darkly, with an eloquence and knowledge far beyond anything I
myself possess. And in my euphoria and pride, which I had vowed
in prayer that very day to vigilantly guard against, I could hardly
wait, when young, to show my poem to someone. And I was
ashamed. Not so much now. Now I feel a quiet awe, and don't feel
like I'm damned and banished forever from illumination. I shrug. I
say aloud, *Look,* under my breath, *look what a big important fly I am,*
and laugh a little, and probably look like a lunatic. Soon none of this
will matter very much, lost in a river of unknown names. I slowly
look up, snow swirling around me. So many poems—a handful are
good enough. The very best resemble one of these snowflakes, this
one right here, so large I can clearly count its six points; it has come

to rest on my sleeve a moment after its long bewildering fall, only to
vanish.

> This snow falling
> On my bedclothes—even this
> comes to me from the pure hand.

AFTER ISSA

AFTERMATH

I stand at the window and look a long time at the heavily snow-laden
pine branches. Glaring blue sky, disturbing after the solace of the
snowstorm, wrapped in its silvery secrecy all night. I can't get over
it . . . *Not today,* says the nurse. *We can tell you that you're going to but
we can't say when,* says a pimply MD. *Everyone is dying,* my friends
say sadly; they all say they'll pray for me, backing farther and farther
away until they are lost from sight. I feel light for a while. Here
we all are together again, on this planet all penitentiary, death row
born and bred. Have you ever noticed the way the solitary and the
disturbed make a special point of avoiding one another, as though
doing so made them invisible, or they stood a better chance out in
the open, vulnerable, without allies. They should all get together,
that's what I think. Because as it turns out—and I know people
find this difficult to believe—I am one of them. We're contagious,
did you know that? And dangerous. Viciously aggressive! Oh, yes!
Dangerous as in a half-crushed worm. And how hard it is to pretend
to be in the same world as everyone else, to have to constantly
pretend to be the person they all used to know. I know the night is
going to walk in my front door one day, and take my hand, and finally
it will be over with. It is only going to come back, the sickness—it
always has, and it would continue to, always. Sickness so familiar,
just like going home. Going home and sitting on the couch with
the two remaining members of my family—there used to be two.
So there we sit mutely in a row on the couch staring straight ahead
and smiling as if we were about to have our picture taken. Yes, I
know all about the condition. And sometimes I wish I had the name
and address of somebody else suffering from it nearby. By the way,
I have been meaning to ask: is that a far off soundless blinding

detonation, a second morning star, or is a poet dying on your block?
Because I would go there and visit him, embrace him, though I
knew I risked badly frightening this person, intruding on a way of
life no company can comfort, no words console, not from above not
from next door.

THOUGHTS OF AN ABANDONED FARMHOUSE

And not to face death with such dread, not to take it so personally. It's nothing, nothing but the force you exert all your life to exclude it from your thoughts that confronts you, when it does arrive, as the horror of being excluded. That got me their attention. The Canadian wind coming in off Lake Erie rattling the windows, forcing the front and back doors. That got them my attention, and I looked up; but I can't understand how I managed it as I had not lived there for decades, and was at the moment a very long ways from there. That's right. I wasn't there at all, and neither was that other bearing my name, poor Christ-haunted child davening slowly in front of me, spider at work on its primer in a far off corner of the known universe shrunk to the dimensions of this house I had not stepped foot outside of for several months, horizontal snow hour after hour. All the black highways that once led to your door deleted . . . Let's try not to worry about it too much. It's just one day out of your life, like any other—and one moment of that day.

Within my heart is a bright ceilingless space, and I have been there. Evening or dawn, first stars or last, I couldn't tell you, hidden path through the forest my height which gives way, between one step and the next, to the dunes, it's coming back to me, endless, identical dunes in their muted otherplanetary light. I turn around. The trees are gone. This is where it begins; it's the same every time. Mirror mirror in the mirror who's living with a gun to his head? Endless hallways of doors without numbers, without doorknobs for that matter. What can you do but keep walking toward that distant pinpoint of light, praying that it doesn't go out, or the blood-dyed thread prove too short, may silver scissors sleep. I am so tired, and I don't know why. I can't go back, I would never make it. Besides, there's no time. I am late, unforgivably late for the wedding, the rhyme of the one who has actually been there but cannot remember a thing and the one who vividly remembers a place she has never been; late for the kiss, the kill, the wood's owl come home at last, the embrace of two people on opposite shores of the ocean. Of things as they should be divided by things as they are.

And talk about being at the right place at the right time. I have always been there, and it's going to end now, no matter how cunning the route, how agile the evasive maneuver. Bang. And so what. So what if there is nothing left of me but this shattered wraith or facsimile of the person who continues, even now, to go by my name. I made it, and that is the one thing I will not be denied. And I urge you to give this some thought. *You have a mind until you use it.* At this point I can barely string together two coherent thoughts or get my shirt buttons in the right holes. But I am still here. Aren't I? I ask if I am here, therefore I am here—but there's no one to ask. And it's very important I know! I feel I am present at the hour I was born for, destination and origin in one. This is the part where I'm supposed to wake up, and I do not wake up. Sudden wind through the leaves that aren't there, the very air turning greener from one instant to the next, and an absolute stillness, even the birds silenced, the birds who aren't there with their eyes closed, and night come in broad daylight. For the Father is coming, the tiger, the whirlwind, the unanswering sky as well as the caryatid who has fallen beneath its stone for good. He lays me out asleep and plunging his hand in my flesh as in mercury, as in melted-down mirror, he pulls the heart from its socket, and truly, it has been hurting me most of my life. A new heart is set in its place, incorruptible, heart of the one with no name or a new name, name so conspicuously alien I'm afraid it is bound to cause no end of strife at recess. By now the wound in my chest's healing over like water into which a millstone has been dropped, still silver water or wide windblown with shimmering path beginning and ending at his feet: love itself, or love unreturned. Meanwhile Abraham, knife raised, is let off the hook at the last minute and later on the mysterious Lord sends his own child to slaughter. Now there is a book I keep meaning to read again, cover to cover the way I did as a boy. If I could only get out of bed, if only I could break these restraints which after all aren't really there. This is where I can always be found, repeating from beginning to end the terrific reasons for being alive, and it's getting us nowhere. How about a story. There once was a man who dreamed he walked to Heaven. And bending down to pick a tiny eye-blue flower from the grass, he woke to find himself holding that flower in his hand! I know just how he felt. Only now I appear to be moving, I am flying at incalculable speeds which continue increasing until finally there is no sensation of motion at all. I am traveling away from my body in widening rings.

NIGHT WINDS

Nude footprints at evening, in August, commingling and rapidly vanishing toward me across the scarlet water, noir. And from moment to moment continuing to darken toward the boundary of night and last light, deep sleep and a dawning awareness of being asleep . . . From lake to land they step with no more effort than it takes to get off a horizontal escalator. Each evening I waited in the blond shade of that ancient yellow willow, swaying and sieving, in the faint stench of drowned fish, pale bellies swollen to the moon; I waited in the moon with one star shining where it wasn't, masterful massé of starlight curving around the fields of lunar gravity. They crowded around me, each in turn reading my face with her cool hands, before hurrying on. All except for one who stayed behind and stood facing me suddenly and gazing past my shoulder as though through the sky. So much younger than I yet she was here before I ever breathed and will be here when I am not, this ghost of future dusks, this disappearing wind more real than I am. I was fifteen the last time I stood here, and unlike hers my face has changed. It's changed a lot, beyond all recognition, and failing to recognize it as anyone alive here now, affectionate hands read my face briefly, gently, before she turns away and hurries on.

THE KISS, 2

The look of love gravely embracing the look of goodbye. In a black-and-white park of bare elms that have the look of elms nobody's looking at. Let's dress them in long scarlet woolens for better visibility as the light is very poor there. And the mystery remains—which is which? Who leaves first? And will they be seeing each other again? Notice there's only one suitcase between them, one passport containing no picture name or gender, no date of birth, only a plausible death day in green, beautiful wind-riffled grass-green. Five or six colorless braille bills in not especially large denominations snugly tucked inside it but with a tendency, like that of clock or compass, to lose their value, their very meaning as you near'd the frontier, the border between this chill but companionable blue filled with the faraway cries of gulls and that infinite black and unbreathable space. The language was shockingly easy to master; it was more like remembering something than learning it. Within a matter of hours they found themselves conversing with effortless fluency. Yet many questions remain unanswered. It's dusk, we know that much; I'm not quite sure how but we do. But does this mean it will soon be light out or night? I vote for light, blindly, on principle. And I think I must be right. Just look. The besieging army whose dawn fires ought to be stretching away to the horizon on every side has stealthily packed up on the very eve of victory, and after so many years of the usual futile and meaningless carnage, departed shadowily without making a sound in the night, as though it was they who'd been under siege—no more. No more unheralded entries through the main gate of one more mute city of ghosts, the wood's owl in its homeward flight so swift it is, can barely be seen, threading unerringly as though predestined a passage between the dense pines—the wood's owl has come home.

1

Suddenly it was finished, how did that happen? He glanced at his watch for some reason. Then he got ready for bed. Outside the wind was blowing. But no sooner had he fallen asleep than the words he had just written began to stir, sluggishly at first, then a little faster. At that point they appeared to careen into a state of panic, dashing blindly up and down and back and forth across the page like ants— ants without purpose or direction, cut off from the current that tells them how to live, and why, and where to go, and what to do when they get there . . . Now most of them were moving in circles, each following closely the one directly in front of it. Elsewhere, a couple head-on collisions occurred. And some found themselves outside the page altogether. Rapidly tapping their forelegs like black canes, soon they were headed in every direction at once until at last the page was left completely blank.

2

He woke and lay perfectly still, like someone attempting to create the impression that he was fast asleep. Finally he opened his eyes, continuing to lie where he was without moving, and thinking about what he'd written. He wished that he could have been clearer. It was all so clear to him. So he was twice alone. But he was living twice.

Wrap it up, he ordered; for some reason he glanced at his watch. Then he undressed and climbed into bed. The wind outside was still. Several hours passed and he opened his eyes. And on the whole he was pleased to be awake again, although he had never been good at it and found it so painful and strange.

PACKAGE

It came finally, this afternoon; intact to all appearances, it gave no indication of having been tampered with. It arrived by sled, oddly enough. I found it odd; but so what? Is it my job to understand everything? It will all be explained. The day is coming when all will be explained. I feel very cheerful about this. It will come to me. When the time is right. I have always been able to feel the reality of this. I feel it and believe it. I am faithful, I can wait. Trembling slightly, I placed the package—how heavy it was for an object so small—in the center of the dining room table. And it must have been then, as I was taking a couple steps back, the better to adore it, I first noticed it giving off a light, a pale blue light, so faint you might easily think it was something you were just imagining. How glad it would have made you. How I wish you had been here. I would have been able to say no you're right, I see it too. Later you can never really talk about a thing like that. As soon as you start to, it changes, don't you think? I don't like to say this, but I don't think it would have happened at all if most of the people I've known in my life had been present. I can't say it exactly amazed me, at that strange hour, alone like that, not having spoken to anyone for what seemed like weeks, not having slept for days, so anxiously had I awaited this moment and for so long. Something told me to leave it alone for now, untouched, unmarred, something to look forward to when I was done with work that day at dawn. It would have made you so glad. The package. The faint blue light—it would have made you so glad to see it. I must have stood there a long time, unable to move. How tired I was. I'd been hoping for a chance to lie down and rest a few hours, to dream again how long it had been, to dream, no longer exist as myself for ten minutes, to be no one at all, no one, a nameless soul at one with God's, with no memories, no plans, no desires, long before death and the knowledge of death overshadowed the planet, of its subsequent conquest by fear, the great ventriloquist, who kept it on from its unknown shadowy throne, to serve as its government of marionettes—poorly considered as it turns out—the time that must have gone into untangling individual legislators and their various coteries with their lynch mob attempts and their meaningless suicides . . . It was only by way of an unbroken chain of work days, of work days and nights of groping refusing to go back and following desolately the miracle in its dark glory through all its lies and illuminations. Does it seem to be dark in here all the time? I could barely make it back to my desk, its surface grown so immense I could no longer catch a glimpse of its end curving away into a haze I would never reach, no matter how far we came, or fast we ran . . . I was so exhausted, maybe I'd already died without knowing it. For it was I who had pulled the sled, the real driver dead, the corpses of the other dogs contributing heavily to my ordeal as, unlashed and unguided, I tried to make out the whispering, words torn from lips still moving in whiteout blizzard for a thousand miles, the ghost body at a desperate sprint. I don't know if it was weeks or years. Without food, without hope, star that had led me here hidden, with nothing, nothing to sustain me but the sight of you waiting, safely, far from pain, far from me, traveler in a far country . . . ; nothing but sitting here watching you lying asleep all in white, so far away. But when am I going to join you? When will we awake?

On the fragments in the appendix: I have always wanted to publish a
book of aphoristic short, even fragmentary pieces that work entirely
by unparaphrasable suggestion. Char's *Leaves of Hypnos,* though it
came out of a very different situation in life, is like my scripture in
this desire.

—FRANZ WRIGHT

*

*The appendix comprises work from the author's last files, including digital
and typed pages, handwritten notes, marginalia, and self-recorded audio.
Wright's term "Unfinishables" encompasses the once-abandoned draft
and the once-finished piece both, frequently exemplified by that material
which upon reworking yielded an intractable, perpetually renewed claim
on his attention—to itself and to the art.*

—E. WRIGHT

APPENDIX: BURIAL HERBS

Fragments & Unfinishables

You strike a match to light
your lamp. But what is lit provides
no light. It is far, far from you that
the circle illuminates.

—RENÉ CHAR

My whole allegiance is to the unwritten poem.

*

The last step cannot be taken by those who have despaired of it: wait until descent is the pretext for continuous ascent.

(AFTER RILKE)

*

I hear the axe is in bloom once more.

I pray because I don't know how not to pray . . .
From the far off blue mountain forests I hear
the axe as it strikes the
silence. then the axe, then
the silence
me.

*

The unconscious is literal-minded.

Let him remain in a condition of listening write down only what
is heard on the part of the conscious mind; just enough to form
simple declarative sentences. The matter, the context of the sen-
tences, verses, etc.—measure of their [illegible]

mind let go of and depart from the material be in other words blank

Words as place to him, when he was lost, where he was homeless of
a world. The *red wind,* say. The words as shield, or spell enough to
make the world survivable another day, and even offer glimpses of a
higher one. As long as he was theirs to use, he thought he could go
on a while, *the red wind,* awe restored, this power to see the mystery
in things restored again, an instant of that now and then, no more,
and this was all he asked of them—if he gave up everything else—
because without it he was certain he would spend life acting like he
wasn't dead. This was all he asked them in return: mystery of things
restored without which he would not have lived. The red wind: it's
doubtful someone else on earth is thinking in unison with him
these words; double doubtful that someone is reading the words
on a page—not under his name. Because they cannot have them
anymore.

The red wind, what's it have to say, the midnight blue still-starry
dawn wind—

If you listen intently enough

The dusk, the red wind, midnight blue more and more starless
dawn wind

If you listened intently enough, if you were patient and blessed with
visits from a condition of stillness both mental and physical—if
you could bring yourself to steal from your employer ten to twenty
consecutive minutes—all right, borrow them—honest to God,

we would bring them right back, no one would even notice they were
missing

Anvil-colored cloud

Weightless anvil

Dawn-gray, aircraft-carrier-gray

To me the words *the red wind* are a place

To me the phrase *the red wind* is a place

*

Amazing—we can never, never not have been here.
Whether anyone knows it or not—and even after no one's here at all!

*

The three or four quick consecutive tugs
on a line long forgotten
in your sleeping
left hand
so that you suddenly wake up
without knowing why.

*

beginning to dream at the wheel

*

Outside the leaves are as quiet as their shadows.
The shade they cast.

When you walk into the room it grows slightly brighter with a warm
low golden color I associate with your voice.

I become happier and more intelligent

*

The imagination & the body sitting down at the same table

Like a child's vision of paradise

*

The seen body as seed of the unseen
The seen body as seed
of the unseen
body

*

but still unborn at heart
still non-existent at heart

*

writing in the dark,
a completely locked door
with the dark on

*

I am an oak with a man's shadow.

*

In my final months I finally broke down and agreed the poem was worth the sound of children crying in an empty house.

*

We're surrounded by things that are over hap-
pening. That are over before they ever happened.

The poor threadbare present—
you can practically see right through it
in certain spots

*

It's like a death, but
there's no body there
to mourn

Poem that nobody wrote

*

Why should the universal experience
be the one I take so personally

*

Nothing theoretical or mystical about it
only some horror-tinged practicalities

*

black hole the size of a period

*

As the surface of the water in a glass very very slowly evaporates so I
am on my knees to give you (back) my ascending, changing face—

(AFTER RILKE)

*

We spent our lives here,
but what were we buying

CAMOUFLAGE

Deep in the *Constitution*
there is a small room (floor
ceiling and walls
all painted red) where
the amputations took place.
A soundproof room

ENGLISH AS A SECOND LONELINESS

1 *Detoxification*

It would be a lie, a transparent and unnecessary lie, to repudiate or
repent of my drug use and its irreversibly ruinous consequences in
my present life and during all the years of my life to come. It gave
me many of my finest and most exalted hours.

And I have been wondering: will I ever use drugs again.

I will if my work wants me to.

And if *it* wants me to.

2 *The Funeral of Childhood*

Did you know not a single person attended the funeral? I think it's
a horrible shame, and I'd like to know what the hell is going on. I
didn't even know it was sick. Not that sick. Didn't you hear people
talking about it, come across an obituary someplace? Nothing! Don't
look at me. If I had known I would have been there. Had my place
at the edge of the grave all staked out, with lawn chair, cooler, sun
umbrella, long before the first light, and I hope that would go with-
out saying. Don't you think it does? I would have looked like quite
a fool, too, evidently, sitting there all by myself through the service.
What is wrong with everyone! I don't even know where it's buried. I
thought I asked you not to look at me.

3 *The Kill*

If anyone persisted in doing to me what I had routinely been doing
to myself for days, months, years on end sometimes, I suppose
sooner or later measures would have to be taken. The hunter is

scented! The prey now slowly, soundlessly moving around behind
him in ever tightening rings.

All out, swift, and massively decisive measures.

4 *Admonition*

You'll wake and wage
your little
page
Say
No
to the pornography of sadness.
To any special pleading based on madness.
No to all potential instances in which
the person you kill and
the person who kills
you are one

5 *Neophyte*

What'll it be this black April morning, snowed the walnut bough—
notebook or rope?

6 *Cause of Death*

As she was cautiously driving along at a speed perfectly appropriate
to that stretch of highway, it appears quite a large, perhaps salmon-
size sperm cell crashes through her windshield, out of a clear blue
sky, ending up under her blankets squiggling there beside her,
meanwhile emitting a series of brief high-pitched squeals which
bring her quite naturally to the verge of psychosis, the heart attack

getting longer, the scream more unheard until at last the ambulance arrives. She will be damned if she is going to "seek help." Nor will she say a word about how it makes her feel, allude to it at all, even in the most peripheral fashion, during her two or three minutes of therapy every morning when the psychiatrist and his entourage breeze through her locked door and right out the window, the blood in her veins turning now into cold molten lead from various meds stabilizing her mood until she has no mood at all, strapped down and ready for takeoff, a method first perfected at this world-famous institution, this is not the time for conventional methods, which might prolong the conflict for years to come and cost the lives of additional countless human beings some of whom aren't even born yet, in the process.

7 *Scientific Method*

Who prays for the ones in the group nobody prays for?

Who prays for those who don't pray for anyone?

8 *English as a Second Loneliness*

Well let's see, I've been doing some teaching. Nothing very exciting I'm afraid. And they do things so differently there, where a semester may go on indefinitely, from cradle to grave in some cases, if the student is rather slow, or simply needs to go at his own pace. We are not all alike are we. We are not machines! It's odd, though, for if, as is true for the vast majority of us the world over, we seem destined to grow up to become just that a small part of greater or lesser significance, of a machine and in so many respects are expected to behave like one, then why not simply face reality & openly prepare children for this near-inevitable eventuality? Why is it that so much

of contemporary education, when you take a couple steps back and
really look the thing over, seems geared to preparing our young for a
world that does not exist at all, not yet, not here? Even at the gradu-
ate level, in the area of fine arts, say, just to choose one at random
from our own culture, hundreds upon hundreds of educators of
unimpeachable morals and even a great affection for the young
and concern for their future lives make an excellent living by lying
to them? Questions better addressed to the great and exceptional
minds of the times—better catch up with one before it's humiliated
or starved to death, driven mad by isolation and solitude.

9 Arctic Bees

Towering and sexless light's personification, messenger, tuner of
tongues, huge cumulus white strap-on wings; being with the golden
lung, hidden in some arctic wood where all bees disappeared from
the earth have built up their own teetering city of hives where
their own sustenance is stored, and food enough for all . . . While
I served forty years as head librarian in a fairy tale concentration
camp whose name I never knew.

SCENES FROM ARLES

The seven foot tall poet

the one who can disappear
merely by standing still
in the wood of words

In the word wood

In the word forest

Forest of words
their shadow
their thing

Forest of the word tree

IN ONE FACE, 1

Dusk wind, red wind . . .

What was it about
to say: I am
the alpha and
I am the omega

The first eyes
to weep
in the world
and the last

One eye
from each face
in one face
gazing
into your eyes

EVERYTHING ELSE WILL CHANGE

Everything on earth
will change when I am dead.
No one will notice but you.
No one will suffer but you.

As my own disappearance was flying
like the shadow of time
across the planet, an arrow
through the night
and the light, a couple hours closer
I was sitting here falling
in love with you,
with an anguish
I cannot describe.
There were so many stories
I had wanted you to hear. But
first I had to tell them to myself.
And this took away from me
thousands of hours, starry hours,
and the green hours I might have spent
doing a few things
to make you happy.
Everything else will change,
your own face will change
into that of someone you have never met,
but this will not change.
What I'm going through
at this very moment
can never be changed.
It cannot be arrested.

It feels like the sun in your chest.
And it can only grow
happier, luckier, vaster,
and younger
and older than you. All at once
overshadowed someday
by a sadness—
five minutes of madness
I don't dare to think about,
you will say I have abandoned you
but think about this,
and remember: it is all so much older
than we are. But look, we are still an us.
And I will never leave you.

Well, I guess this must have been it all along, the museum where "the World's Most Amazing Lost Objects" are on display this week and this week only. I thought we'd never find it! I suppose I must have stopped ten people on the street to ask directions. A worried and fragile-looking child of six in formal white collar finally pointing at a grimy windowless place across the street while staring straight into my eyes, intensely, searchingly, as in a last-chance attempt at conveying without words information whose lack diminished substantially our chances of being around the next day would be substantially diminished with every passing minute. Not much to look at, from the outside. Maybe it was all a mistake, the way it so often was, in any event we were soon bobbing away from one another on separate currents taking us in opposite directions. I had to laugh while I waited for the light to change. Naturally, my destination all these hours was practically next door to the midtown landmark known the world over, that skyscraper made entirely of mirror, rendering it nearly invisible. It made you wonder, What the hell were they all up to in there! But nobody seemed to know, and if they cared, they were doing an unusually brilliant job of concealing it from their fellow citizens. Today, of all days, the building appears to have been taken over by what could only be described as cockroach-like creatures the size of tanks. They had been there all morning long according to the voice of that singular child who was now nowhere to be seen, rolling up and down the defenseless Palace of Baa, Lord, and leaving behind trails of a highly corrosive substance, in color and texture like unto snot. Now I really had to laugh. But where were you supposed to go; what were you supposed to do. Sensing my distress, that admirable child suggested I skip the earlier shows absolutely, and rest and relax today, and return in the evening, which is when all the words people were about to say that day, or intended to say that day, had just been forgotten. From getting to be said, they had, in one of endless ways, gone to being disappointed, frustrated, cut off—this was when they loved to gather by the billions and fly in mad circles, in silence, for utter joy. And right at that moment—what a beautiful morning—he might like to meander along a few blocks and pay our respects at the city's famous university, perhaps pausing a minute to light a candle, or at least think about it, there at that black-scarred trough of the wind and piss-gutted candle butts going back decades, to the left of the illustrious cracked marble stairway that leads to the places where language itself goes every day to learn to die.

FRAGMENTARY HOMAGE

I feel like Philip Marlowe sometimes, lost in his Los Angeles of words, of austere and immaculate syntax, parked on the words street in sight of the ocean at dawn, waiting for the word sun to rise. He gets out of the word car and walks toward the word water, tasting the words a light wind in his face. But the word that represents L.A., even on those days when you can see it, is different from his word for it, vastly different in connotation. How, by the way, can they stand it, the word people? What happened to the word sky, the words mountains to the east? How can they breathe them, the words yellow gas? How long are they going to put up with it, just stand there like the word sheep on the words assembly belt, waiting their turn to have the word skull bashed in or the word throat cut? One day they'll start leaving, little by little; first the words the poor will begin to pack the word suitcases, and a few at a time they'll get out in the idiom on foot, in the phrase never once looking back, in the verb traveling, mostly traveling at the noun night, and passing unnoticed, farther and farther, into the unspoken north.

Dusk wind, red wind—

what is it saying? To midnight blue, minus per second one star; a case of the minus one star yet still starry dawn wind, what was it about to say? I am the Alpha, the Omega; I am the first face that wept, and I will be the last. Detour. Forget about time. In most, defiance ends with a diploma, oh cute little rats baring their teeth, baring their throats, baaing away, sporting colorful electrodes, what the hell; sooner or later, through one illusory wall or another . . . They look so real. Feel. Yes, quite solid, realistic. After a while hardly anyone can tell the difference anymore. Separates the nuts from the shells. He struggles to his feet in another world just about to close. The others stampeding right over him. Sleep. Back to sleep go. And so they enter the next maze, glib orphans of the divine with their sinister toys, those plastic hives of meaningless misinformation strapped to their backs, Magic Marker smiley masks on, left to decay in their Etch A Sketch library shelves: lost in a blizzard of hours spent memorizing television dialogue, their faces smeared with marijuana brownie batter a lovely shade of feces, Christ, they're never going to learn how to think now. On their knees weeping with gratitude for that job at the bank all dressed up as adults in their coffin clothes. Five days a week, the best hours of each of those days spent on the telephone frightening the poor, pretty grueling, almost too worried themselves to speak, those quarter of a million dollar educations down the drain of the receiver's wormholes, startled to see their own phone numbers coming up next . . .

*

. . . with remarkable consistency those who check the box, boxes
which have the appearance (and to tell you the truth they weren't
really boxes at all but perfect parallelograms) of little black
coffins . . .

BLACK AURORAS

1

Entry: March 28, 1979

Now where am I? It looks like the pale gold rooms inside a corn-field. In that corridor of country that parallels Lake Erie. And my old college friend X is walking fifty yards or so directly ahead of me; I notice I have synchronized my footsteps with his so that he cannot hear the crackling underneath my boots as I cross the field. Out of nowhere a dark wall of woods stands before us. He enters the out-skirts of trees and I follow after him, I don't know why. I do know where we are, though: a stone's throw from the small leaden ocean with its surf of three inch waves. X has stopped walking, therefore I have stopped. Now I am standing directly behind him and trying not to move, make a sound, or breathe so that he might feel my breath on the spine of his neck, I am standing that close. He is now reading a book, and I begin to read along.

There are tiny spiders who like to live in books. I saw one, once, reading in the old library stacks where I spent one northern Ohio summer helping to box them up, load them into trucks, and see to it that they were safely unloaded out back of that mistake of a new library. It was a bright translucent green amidst the dust of decades, the color of the first spring leaves, and a bit smaller than an asterisk. I thought it was one until it suddenly moved. X is closely examin-ing the trunk of an ancient dark elm to the left of me. Now he has produced a miniature glass pipe from the inside pocket of his jacket and, with amazing delicacy, taking great care not to harm it, has plucked from the bark of this tree trunk a bark-colored spider and is getting ready to smoke it.

Sarah Scarfield

You wake in the middle of the night. And what the hell are you doing lying on your back in the chilly wet grass of the backyard with a hurricane lamp, yellow-nimbused, sitting next to your head, and lying beside you, pillowed on one out-thrust arm like the neck of an exceptionally skinny young woman, the long handle of a shovel. Suddenly you're on your feet, startled eyes open wide. I don't think I've ever seen a human being move that fast. You slowly turn your head to look around and find your whole neighborhood enveloped in darkness except for one lamplit window way up in the attic of your house; however, where that lit window is shining, no room exists. Does it ever stand out in the night. And the house makes you think of the towering prow of a ship looming over and very slowly bearing down on you. And would you look at that sky. You look up, and there certainly are a lot of stars staring down, very small. You begin counting them as you once tried to so long ago, but it's pointless, isn't it? All this time you have been wandering across the black lawn without thinking about it. And your foot has come in contact with what seems to be a mound of freshly dug earth, though quite a small one. You set the lamp and shovel down and, settling yourself on your hands and knees, run your hand across it. It feels like it's covered with sparse newly sown grass. You begin tentatively burrowing into it and immediately stop. A hard shrunken kernel of corn lies in the palm of your hand like the tooth of a child, a very ancient child. She was buried here in March, a week or so after you were born. And how would you know that? You're asleep, and allowed to know everything.

3

Nursing Home out on Route Unknown

Children age as rapidly as presidents here. And them presidents.
No way. I mean to gauge how hugely they age. (It is the middle of
the night, cricket voices numerous as the stars beyond the ceiling,
a night-light is the only source of light and I lie in my mechanical
bed wide awake.) And failing to outlive everyone that you have ever
known a source of awful shame. And so, desolate and frightened as
I am, too frightened to tell anyone, to speak at all, I lie here await-
ing the long anticipated benefits of my longevity. They have yet to
arrive, but I know they are coming. They must be. I have been lying
here so long I did not notice that I had begun to shrivel up and
shrink until I was the size of a solitary cricket. I feel the bed begin to
quake, a couple of nurses feeling around through the sheets, I hear
them saying in low voices, She's gone God damn it! Mrs. Dement is
gone. No, no, I am here, I am right here I cry in a voice that shocks
me, one that I can barely hear myself. It's no use. I am afraid they
are not coming, and my life as I have known it cannot go on. I hop
to the windowsill, the guillotine of the window hanging far above,
propped open by an old dictionary, and leap, floating down into the
long grass, the darkness, the blue August stars . . .

4

Black Aurora

Throughout my life the great gag among my acquaintances was that
I would live to see them all buried. And my God, I did. And now I
am suffering from what appears to be an incurable case of some
form of flesh-eating rage and humiliation. At the moment I am
being pushed rather roughly in my wheelchair by an enormous and
burly moron in what appears to be a stained white butcher's apron,
across a vast expanse of floor I picture as a chessboard though

it is only the dayroom linoleum and as the evening falls and the
shadows deepen we make our slow progress toward the northeast
quadrant where I will spend the better part of the late afternoon and
evening hours glaring at my reflection in the window and waiting,
waiting impatiently for Mother to come, her cool hands to light on
my shoulders and her lips to touch the wrinkly flaccid gray flesh
of my bald skull, her long black hair flowing and curtaining down
all around me already starry with the scent of main streets after
midnight and the first arctic wind that comes with the last nights of
fall.

It won't be long now, planet of ghosts. I never saw a bedroom like
it. Ghosts past, eventual, and still to come, ceiling on the shadowy
side, otherwise ideal: cozy once you get used to the enormity, dif-
ficult to say just how with this incredible sleepiness rolling over me,
such matters diminishing in importance with each passing second
as I stand in a far northeast corner naked and shivering, shriveled
sex cupped in my hands: as I sit up in my huge down bed floating in
pure resignation to despair, suspended in worldwide affection and
a peace I'd never known that pervades the whole space like a gas. I
looked on just then as my right hand, emaciated beyond recogni-
tion, reached out to switch off the bedside lamp, shade approximat-
ing the size of a thimble, making this no simple operation, and
leaving me surrounded by something the word *darkness* does not at
all convey: darkness not of our darkness, a black dazzling, I can't.
I can't anymore. I think I'd have to bring each one of you with me
in person if what I saw were to be sufficiently conveyed, let me get
some sleep. And if recent statements regarding the sales of my
books are any indication, this plan is far from impracticable: one by
one I'd lead you there and point. You have my guarantee that you,
too, would be struck dumb with astonishment and awe. But let us
not "go there." Each of you is precious to me—I wish I could take
you all out to dinner one evening. For while your kindness, your
magnanimity of spirit, and your practical generosity are never lost
on me, dear elite, and never far from my thoughts, I deem this an
experience best inflicted on close family members and friends. I
think at best there are one or two left, or none at all. None at all . . .
I like the sound of that. There are responsibilities and there are
responsibilities; and while I'm not sure which is which, you see
what I mean, maybe, who cares. Oh I know you do. You'll take it to
your breast. You're not some sort of monsters, are you! For as every-

one knows only too well, one is bound to be severely mauled by that
which haunts the conscience past a certain age, and statistical inevi-
tability tells me that some of you have tasted it. Tend to drift amends-
wise without fail. The narrator is now thoroughly lost and about to
break down and ask directions. Oh yes, close family. Come to think
of it, this option would seem to present its own strategic complexi-
ties. I never really knew them that well, and have not always been
able to keep track of their movements. A strange coincidence: just
the other day I was reading in the newspaper, grown rapidly archaic
in my hands, about their inexplicable disappearance. If they only
knew what a commonplace this is among us, I snickered. But no,
this time it appeared to be permanent. I suspected abduction [finger
pointing upward] or, being of an optimistic bent, ravenous birds.
It was right then I fell into a deep paralyzed slumber. As in sepia
visions I floated past Toledo toward Lake Erie. I drifted like a zep-
pelin made out of cloud-colored marble filled with hushed Germans
over a fiery sea, limitless visibility and ceiling, with only a slight
chance of early warning sirens, rising higher and higher until I was
lost from view, never to return. I woke in my moss armchair, in one
of the innumerable chambers of my mansion underground, weep-
ing like a child. Then I woke in this bed, this time for real, I think I
can say that with some degree of confidence. Family. What a strange
word, *family*. And friends? I guess I misplaced them, let me know if
you come across any of them, will you? Tell them I am having trou-
ble with the new music, which is that it's ugly and let me know what
they think. Let me know when the dead rise and the past returns.
Or we could just forget the whole thing. I can't even remember
what I was getting at, except composing filler for my final essay,
"Circumlocution, Obscurity for Obscurity's Sake, and the Non
Sequitur as Irritating Howl of Envy." All I know is ever since then I
keep hearing these voices suggesting with majestic indifference and
in an undeniably nonpartisan manner that I do things like drink a
small glass of apple juice. I think that was the scariest one. No—it
was the one regarding Brian, our dog, who might need a walk or a

snack, "if he is still alive." But just as I am about to lose my grip on
shared objective reality, that paradise, and succumb at last to sleep's
dark currents swift and deep &c., torn as a last leaf in fall from the
branch right outside the window of the room where a child has
finally left her tortured body; just as I was about to dive, I freeze,
a violet sun shining through my skull like a terrible truth raising
its feathered reptilian head after years of lurking right below the
surface. And I'm afraid that's about the best I can do. I know one
thing. The look of love looks like the look of goodbye. Or vice versa.
Suddenly the whole room was as bright as the one in which I was
born. How does anyone get any sleep around here? Not that it made
much difference now. I was getting pretty used to not shutting my
eyes for the last nearly two years. All for the best. The shock might
have killed me. I might have died before I woke as in the famous
bedtime prayer. A work of sheer psychological genius. No such luck,
chief. As for the perilous effects not dreaming is said to have on the
bodies of man and rat alike—not dreaming? If I'm not mistaken, it
would seem I spent the better part of my life doing just that. Listen,
Mister Obituary Scorecard, you can wake up every day in your nurs-
ing home and prepare to enjoy the wondrous rewards of longevity,
though there may be the absence from the earth of everyone you
ever knew to consider. Nobody will be shedding any tears over you
now. Eyes will glaze over and roll back in their heads the moment
you begin reciting, as though for the first time, the ballad of your
birth in an abandoned bird's nest hidden away deep in the burgundy
dusk, wind-slashing crown of ashen vines, collapsed veins gray and
green, as we lay awake all morning gazing into the sideways bliz-
zard out on the North Dakota farm. Remember? We finally had
to move though. Somebody built a house a hundred miles away;
I lost my mind from the claustrophobia alone. I feel all right now.
Ceaseless whispering continues from deep within my sleep or
under the floor beneath my bed, the look of love looks like the look
of goodbye. If you don't know that, you soon will, if you're lucky.
Oh it won't be long now, planet all death row. Nice big cell you got

there. Planet of nothingness, what if it's true, and there's nothing, and sentience itself some accidental scum growing on the surface of this immeasurable nothingness, the unplanted grain, this mote of murderers and their challenged flocks, this infinitesimal anguish nobody cares about, nobody sees, Place of Hate Everything Fear Everyone nothing nothing nothing. Would that make them happy?

Love your neighbor. Love your stranger. Stranger, love your life.

ON THE OUTSKIRTS OF ARLES

Two rows of tall cypresses divided by a thread-thin stream, a leaden silver or a blue-white liquid diamond, depending on the inclination of the light or width (about 12 feet across here) of the water. The world cannot be saved, a shame, in other words. A shame, in other worlds, but without perceiver—I dream of one without perceiver, without perceiver inadvertently destroying it or quite advertently I fear. Or one with the job of raising it, to the next round, a ray of spirit gazing at. What? Through which mirror or into what window? Who the creator and which the created, who the pregnant killer, who emaciated birther. May you be saved in secret from the world, too much to ask. For who could bear it, being both seer and seen? Each tall slender tree the image of the one across from it, more or less. In the end less. The resemblance more that of a sibling, in some cases a parent, or child; or friend seen alive once again in a dream, in the guise, inexplicably, of some other, this fact only recognized later or noticed but unremarked on at the time. Everybody has this dream, perhaps the great mystery. They create the impression during the windy times of reaching out in order to touch fingertips, mingle, embrace. Or of mute children signing goodbye. Now with their backs to one another. Why say it, why not simply see; why see, and why not sit and simply say? If someone there, to take it down; if broken hands, in total dark. Why, on what is as much a part of who he is as his own body, continuously harp, expatiate, keep silent, store, and for whose sustenance and where—in things seen or word said. In dream we wake to or the world along whose shore (a river there) we wander, unremembering all, unwinding no thread to guide back. Thin stream again, awake, thank God. At bottom, through uncountable pages of water, white sand; one Pleiades-manacled crayfish, absorbed in minute excavations. At bottom one endless and ceilingless cathedral lit a brilliant yellow darkness, at dawn—is it dawn yet, or midnight? It's in the title. To the person hearing or reading, the one I imagine, that one word will say it all. As this page is one word in a book never written, never to be finished, take pity. Between seen sunlight's bee, detonation or a simple flame, space to house the candles they'll make of each one of us yet.

OCTOBER 17, 2012

NIGHT WINDS (ALTERNATE)

Innumerable prints of bare feet commingling and rapidly vanishing away from me over the burgundy water darkening minute by minute, from land to lake they pass without paying attention or anything else. The words *celestial escalator* come to mind. To mine. What about yours? They do now. What is the past? Only a moment ago. I was spoken, before long I'll be decaying, like a note, or the sun. I'm half-disappearing already, first fading from your tongue, then seen on a street corner waiting for a light, among the category of memories and ghosts, fading from view again. And I want to be one of you, flying unseen over failing and darkening memory's sapphire-black waters, fate's coolant, the tears rolling up your cheeks and back into my eyes.

CLEARLAKE OAKS, CALIFORNIA

Brilliant yellow darkness
small intense flames
wavering
as when someone walks past them
and into the past.
Frail scent of honey
even through the veil of heavy incense, pale
wax gradually but inexorably
changing back into daylight.
In the dilating dusk.
Evening's inky chill
rising to the ankles,
knees, and the black face of God
vanishing into the dome above
and the night beyond the dome, leaving
nothing but the great round lupine
eyes like breathed-on coal . . .
I have lost track of my brother.

brilliant yellow darkness, wavering
as though someone had passed by
in the dilating dusk
eyes all pupil
evening rising to your ankles to your knees
the black face of Christ in the dome overhead
(vanishing gold raptor's eyes)

disappeared now except for
its gold raptor's eyes

*

PRAYER

Brilliant yellow darkness, wavering candle flames
of darkness.

AT HIS DESK IN THE PAST

An homage to Karl Krolow

transcribed from self-recorded drafts on audio from January 16, April 13, 14, 19, 21, 2012

FIRST light. It's raining again in a dead language. Green. It's raining in a dead language. Green again. It's raining again in a dead language. Green. The empty and utterly silent house filled all at once with the sound of my name posed, in my young mother's voice before I finally slept. And it rained harder, rains without end, with no beginning; it rains without cease in black and white it shows no sign of ever stopping it rains and it will go on raining with no time no date. I love to sleep when it is raining no meaning and the name of no meaning and the meaning of having no name.

*

HE HAS LIVED a long time. It has happened before. He suddenly heard quite distinctly and apropos of nothing words that enchant him and continue to throughout the day although he could not tell you why or what they mean and wouldn't try. To him they are a place to go different from the ones he knows and very different from the world, which they protect him from and beautify, alone or in the company of others, whether he is well or sick he cannot speak, like someone very moved he cannot speak. That they haunt him he would not know how to say. If he could say, they would be of little use to him; they are always haunting him whether or not he catches them all. The words enchant and make him happy though he would not be able to say yes they also haunt him. That they hurt him as well he would see as completely irrelevant, silent man of the millions of pages words visible still, still traveling toward the world although he is not there, not here, maybe he quietly speaks them

aloud once or twice before writing them down and feels strangely
blessed.

*

IT'S RAINING in a dead language he writes at his desk in the
past, silent man of the millions of pages still traveling toward the
world—no— no

*

SILENT MAN of the millions of pages, words still traveling toward
the world although he is not there although he is not here or any-
where. Maybe he quietly speaks them aloud once or twice before
writing them down and feels strangely blessed.

*

IT'S RAINING in a dead language he writes at his desk in the past,
silent man of the millions of pages; words come or are given to
him even now, words more real a place to him than one they might
depict or any place on earth itself or thing there they might rep-
resent, world where things are words that soundlessly pronounce
themselves, six words more real to him, unbidden, no thought
taken and apropos of absolutely nothing they have come once more
to the man of the billions of words.

*

WORLD where things are words that pronounce themselves
soundlessly with no assistance from him, six of the words that still
come to him not stamped as black on one side of six shining white
cubes of the random or blocks the size of his head arranged and

rearranged as many times as it would take in total dark to thread a
needle each day: dawn still found him there.

*

AS JEWELS dark and bright haunting beyond price as pearls so
translucent and light in the palm of his hand that it doesn't exist,
almost—hand that staggered out once more to meet head-on its
disappearance, pearl left spinning in mid-air.

*

AND we'd do it again wouldn't we—every last one of us choos-
ing precisely what we had been given, a glimpse of a night sky—
no—choosing precisely what we had been given not to be a sky
of infinite diamonds unaware they live forever or exist at all but a
pair of mortal eyes with the glory to see them, grieving their loss, a
glimpse.

*

DURATION: silent lightning, altitude minus six feet north by north
north each dark blue fir's tall frozen flame

*

ROW of slender tapers made by melting down of the endless hexa-
gon. Flames of a bright solar darkness right next to a row of those of
a dark yellow brightness replaced in eight minute waves by a dotted
line of bees traveling down one of the twelve spokes of hallway mak-
ing an abrupt right angle turn it travels toward the right eye of the
icon entrance and preserves the words there.

*

ROW of slender tapers each requiring the melting down of a precise
but undivulged number of hexagonal cells identical immaculate
bee-light the icon the bees in the icon rows of slowly dwindling or
weeping rows of slowly

*

WAXING tapers—no—rows of slowly dwindling

*

WANING tapers—no—rows of slowly

*

DWINDLING tapers bright solar darkness or dark yellow brightness
one weeping taper bee-light the bees in the icon

*

IT'S RAINING in a dead language he rapidly writes in the notebook
he carries so rapidly he might be wrapping up an interview with
a flash of black lightning that the notebook might be back in its
pocket and his hands casually folded before anyone notices that he
is gone

*

NORTH by north north present altitude minus six feet

*

SPEECHLESS man to whom they speak or maybe for whom, hive
where they lived and where what they'd produced out of their brief
lives lay stored up, again he tasted

*

A HUMMING the distant vibration that's heard in the hand placed
lightly on the feverish infant's forehead in ear or lips lightly pressed
to its brain the knitted fontanelle, his own skull a lone Golgothan
crystal helping constitute the Andean or lunar Salt Lake City flats
prisming one of sidereal reaction too vast for all the eight billion
minds blinking mortally on and off to hold at this begraced time
one mortal source of light bearably visible so far it may no longer be
there in the heaven of the dark along with so many identical others
that live longer than we can conceive although not long enough for
God to give each one a name

*

PERPETUALLY mirrored in so many eyes evolved for this purpose,
why?

*

OR IN THE SIDEREAL mirror of the ocean where they will
bequeath their tear before they go?

*

TO THIS BRAIN or desert hive this named mind or single roaring

*

TEAR OF OCEAN, one ocean for each eye

*

OR SOLITARY MOUNTAINTOP observatory and that distant
humming sound it made opening and closing in the one moment
in time immeasurable as his death's or conception's as the space
between them the space in time required to take in all the stars and
their identical name

*

TO THE HUMMING response of the words in their closed books
all around him, the evening dark deepening beginning to pool at his
ankles, and in his mind a moment he is a boy of six

*

HE SMELLS AGAIN the faint honey scent dust and incense speech-
lessly he feels the loneliness of tapers as the stained glass turns to
black; they wane in there alone with no company but him and his
mother and fueling the small brilliant radius of fire that auras vary-
ing altitudes of fire and honey-colored irises of icon eyes that follow
unseen beings, muted wings of invisible gold iridescent as they
gravely

*

BEE-iridescent

*

THEY WANE in there alone with no company but him and his
mother and fueling the small brilliant radius of fire that auras vary-
ing altitudes of fire and honey-colored

*

OF FLAME and holly-colored irises of icon eyes that follow unseen
beings muted wings of invisible gold bee-iridescent as they gravely

*

SYSTOLICALLY wave, the messengers come and their tongues are
of flame these *tuners of lungs* hovering above the brimming sub-
stance made from sunlight by bees, creatures they were given to
contribute to creation the waning of their secret names the silent
weeping of their diminishing

*

OF THE MOTHER'S shadowy face in profile the only way he dares
to picture her at all, nameless at his birth hour identical twin to the
hour of her death

*

NOT ONE tear melting down her cheek even if a thawing comes
and he can feel again there in the bright yellow dark, the dark yellow
light, dazzled darkness of eyes that never weep though constantly
brimming though a humming comes forever from far voices down
brain hallways from mind-shadows thrown on the high walls of that
place

*

COMPLETELY flooded with this dim radiant dusk all the way to the dome of that human hive forever storing up Christ's eyes ultimate altitude forever gazing down into their minds, face farther and farther and more immense as walls and ceilings recede into the boundaryless air

*

AND THE HUMMING may just be the man

*

AS HE QUIETLY SAYS THE HEXAGONAL sentence aloud barely breathing silently reciting

*

EACH WORD of it once before writing it down, feeling blessed, and once more before giving it back.

THE PEAK

At eight I made a city disappear, along with
my one friend

there, for the first time. Two more major
cities had met the

same fate by the time I'd turned twelve (and
resolved, impla-

cably, to make no further friend). I'd
learned. I heard a voice

say, Would it be ok to just lie here, turn
to the wall, and die?

"No it would not," I said, and got up. And
there I stood. Hard

to breathe, hard to combat complete
annihilation by a solitude

that endless and blue, arctic clouds like
icebergs or vast ineluc-

tably altering faces of marble drifting
past—I could have reached

out and touched them, if there had been
something to touch.

I felt my upturned forehead scoured, my very
name effaced,

and whatever was left of me polished until
it beamed. What-

ever about me no longer hurt, possessed a
history, a future, or

the most infinitesimal hope.

Notes & Acknowledgments

Special thanks to *The New Yorker* and *The Nation*, where "Favor" and "Night Winds (alternate)," respectively, originally appeared. Thanks also to the editors of *Poetry* magazine, where the following poems originally appeared: "Akechi's Wife," "Boardinghouse with No Visible Address," "The Break," "The Raising of Lazarus," and "The Rule."

Some of these poems and/or previous versions of these poems have appeared in the following journals: *Comment Magazine* (Toronto), *Drunken Boat, Free Verse, Gulf Coast: A Journal of Literature and Fine Arts, Laurel Review, Lincoln Review* (UK), *Pebble Lake Review, Pleiades, Poetry, Prairie Schooner, Sargasso* (Germany), and *Triggerfish Critical Review.*

A number of poems have appeared in chapbooks published by Argos Books, Back Pages Publishers, Foundlings Press, Marick Press, Tungsten Press (Netherlands), and Zinnbooks (Germany).

The following notes are contributions by the author except where otherwise indicated.

*

I would like to establish that most of these poems are, in one way or another, addressed to or about my wife, and that without her assistance, verging at times on coauthorship, none of these poems could have been written at all. And as spouses of authors are frequently credited with similar feats, I feel it necessary to state that in the case of my book this claim is, I suspect, made with more than customary literalness as it was written during a period in my life characterized by more than customary disability, which is saying something.

"Telepathy flowing between us like water" in "In Lieu of Rent" was inspired by the notes and letters of William Burroughs. —EOW

Alcoholocaust, in the penultimate line of "In Lieu of Rent," was brilliantly coined by Malcolm Lowry in a letter to a friend.

"The Raising of Lazarus" is the final version based loosely on a fragment of Rainer Maria Rilke unpublished in the poet's lifetime. The first version I completed while in college in 1977; it later appeared in *The Unknown Rilke* (Oberlin College Press).

"The Kiss" 1 and 2 are both versions, greatly expanded, based on five lines by René Char which I have been working on for decades.

"The Kiss" (1 & 2), "The Writing" (1 & 2), and "The Lamp, 2" reflect the author's practice of revising a poem written in verse as a prose piece and vice versa, going back and forth between the two, exploring their particular influence, a practice concerned less with avoiding repetition across the two versions than with rediscovering and responding to each form's inherent tendencies. The original title with number remains as per author predating the order of contents and indicates simply that there exists a matching title written in verse or prose. The prose counterpart to "Lamp" is published in the author's previous volume of poetry F. —EOW

The six-word line "It's raining in a dead language," first appearing in Wright's poem "First Light," was inspired by the line "Rain like/too-long sentences/in a dead language . . ." found in the translation into English by Stuart Friebert from the German of the poem "Regen" by Karl Krolow. Wright spoke of the importance of the words to him: "it has haunted me and infuriated me that I did not write it and made me sick with envy since I was an undergraduate." (Franz Wright voice file: 120714_007 @0:17. Wright private collection) —EOW

The Issa version within "Haiku Written on the Verge of Death" is supposed to be the last poem the elderly haiku master composed, apparently after being carried by stretcher from his burning house during a snowstorm.

"Thoughts of an Abandoned Farmhouse" begins with a loose rendering of a passage in Merleau-Ponty's *Phenomenology of Perception*. A similar version was published in *Ill Lit* under the title "Thoughts of a Solitary Farmhouse."

The second fragmentary piece appearing in the appendix was constructed by the author from his versions of lines isolated from poems by Paul Celan ("I Hear"), Czesław Miłosz ("An Alcoholic Enters the Gates of Heaven"), and Rainer Brambach ("The Axe"), in that order. The third and ultimate lines are his additions. —EOW

A NOTE ON THE TYPE

This book was set in Scala, a typeface designed by the Dutch designer Martin Majoor (b. 1960) in 1988 and released by the FontFont foundry in 1990. While designed as a fully modern family of fonts containing both a serif and a sans serif alphabet, Scala retains many refinements normally associated with traditional fonts.

Composed by North Market Street Graphics,
Lancaster, Pennsylvania

Designed by Soonyoung Kwon